God On
Death Row

Michael Nadraus

Copyright © 2005 Michael Nadraus
All rights reserved. No part of this publication may be reproduced, stored in a retrieval system, or transmitted in any form or by any means, electronic, mechanical, photocopying, recording, or otherwise, without the prior written permission of the publisher.

ISBN: 0-9769186-4-1

Published by:
Holy Fire Publishing
531 Constitution Blvd. Martinsburg, WV 25401
www.ChristianPublish.com

Cover Design: Jay Cookingham

Printed in the United States of America and the United Kingdom

Dedication

This book is dedicated to every inmate on death row & in prisons & jails across the country that corresponds with me. The Whalers, Jayson Toth, Crystal & Patty, Jordan, Vince, Ronaldo, Tiana, Fallon & Maureen, Anthony the Penguin & ALL the rest of the Kings Kids of Bayview Baptist Church, Mike Buscemi Rudolph, Judson 101 (Dennis Rew, Phil Carroll, Fatty Matt Pankratz), Miller & Terpstra, MBBC Prison Ministry, Chaplains Waaland & Peleck, Cook County Jail, Leon & Sharon, Jamie Konzelmon, Zeman & Amanda Toth & last but not least Kevin QB Taylor.

www.godondeathrow.com

God on Death Row

Table of Contents

Introduction		page 7
Chapter 1	Methods of Execution	page 11
Chapter 2	Where's Your Faith	page 15
Chapter 3	Michael McBride	page 17
Chapter 4	Orion Joiner	page 19
Chapter 5	Leo Little	page 21
Chapter 6	Leon Lawrence	page 31
Chapter 7	Pam Perillo	page 43
Chapter 8	Clay Smith	page 47
Chapter 9	Jeff Dillingham	page 69
Chapter 10	Greg Wright	page 73
Chapter 11	Susan Atkins	page 75
Chapter 12	Julius Murphy	page 81
Chapter 13	Wayne Wesbrook	page 87
Chapter 14	Jordan Crystal	page 101
Chapter 15	John Burks	page 105
Chapter 16	David Goff	page 107
Chapter 17	Calvin McGee	page 109
Chapter 18	David Berkowitz	page 111
Chapter 19	Jeffrey Dahmer	page 137
Chapter 20	Charles Manson	page 141
Chapter 21	Timothy McVeigh	page 153
Chapter 22	Biblical O.T. Death Penalty Sins	page 155
Chapter 23	What States Kill You & What States Don't	page 157
Chapter 24	Texas Leads the Way (facts & figures)	page 159
Chapter 25	100% True Inmates Stories	page 163
Chapter 26	Salvation	page 181
Chapter 27	Reaching Out	page 183

GOD ON DEATH ROW

By Michael Nadraus

Introduction:

    Death Row is currently the home to almost 4,000 inmates. Day after day they sit in a cell waiting for their appointment with death, the dreaded execution date. On that day they meet one of these five dooms: lethal injection, electrocution, hanging, firing squad or the gas chamber. Some are innocent of the crimes they are accused of committing, but many are hopelessly guilty of murder.

    This book explains and tells the tales of many of the inmates on death row from all over the United States. Over the last few years I have been working with over 250 inmates sentenced to death and other various serial killers. I consider myself blessed to have made the friends I now have in the inmate population. Interaction with an inmate goes a long way. Letters can mean a world of difference to them. A visit can brighten up their whole month. I wasn't sure at first what to expect when I began corresponding with death row inmates, but it has proven to be a fulfilling experience. The letters sent to me from killers and some innocent inmates have been collected and compiled to help answer this question in their own words: "Is God on Death Row?"

    Death row was renamed Life row by Karla Faye Tucker a few years back. Death row is not the end of the journey for these inmates but it is the beginning of one. Faith in God helps many of them get through the ordeal. Some outsiders call it 'prison religion' or in other words a religious awakening that is fake and only created to impress or fool guards and others around them. Prison religion is a real thing but it would be foolish to think it was the only kind. There is true genuine repentance and faith found in prison. God is real and alive today. Each letter in this book is a testament to that fact of changed lives and eternities all due to Jesus Christ and what he did on the cross.

    From the creation of Heaven and the earth to the reinstatement of the death penalty in 1976, God has been there. This book will take you on a journey from childhood to inmate to death. The writings of these men on death row come from the heart and soul of each one. The honest truth is poured out on paper and awaiting a hungry reader. Last statements made minutes before the time of execution bear facts and good-byes from the depths of their lives. Death row is a place unlike anywhere else in the world. You can break your business appointments. You can break your dentist appointments. But the one thing we all have in common is our appointment with death and judgment. The only difference between death row inmates and us is they know the day and time they are going to meet their Maker.

The moment these men are locked down in their cell for the first time is the moment many of them realize that they have lost control over it all. Some cry their eyes out, and some sit in silence for days lingering on the thoughts of the past months. Some even give thanks to God for being where they are. No two men on death row are alike. They are like snowflakes, each different in their own way. As the state tries to mold them into what they think they should be, the inmates of strong character maintain their personalities and courage.

Does throwing them in the dungeon make amends? What goes on in the middle of the night on death row? What would they do in the first 24 hours of freedom if they were pardoned? What keeps them sane? How good does it feel to forgive? What about their souls as they enter eternity? Why can a drug user go to rehab and become rehabilitated and people accept it, yet if you kill someone, people think there is no rehabilitation? The gripping words penned by these men will explain these questions and many more in powerful detail as you never imagined. Welcome to death row!

Sometimes these inmates lose both their hope and focus on life. Some sit and imagine pianos and symphonies in their minds, so real they can hear them. Some pretend to be free, and others give up and commit suicide.

It can make me wonder sometimes. I truly hate to get up and go to work some days when it is beautiful outside. I hate to have plans outside and then it rains. What would these inmates on death row give to go outside on a rainy day or to get up and actually go to a job each day? It can make you cherish the freedoms you have, the freedom of being able to come and go as you please and not be trapped in the same 6' by 9' cell basically the rest of your life. All this is something practically all of these men and women will never have again.

Wanting 15 minutes of fame still lies deep within the hearts of many inmates who have done small crimes but are locked up for many years. The legendary killers such as Charles Manson, John Wayne Gacy and Jeffrey Dahmer all have been targets of inmates who seek the fame of being the one who killed the legend. It seems that the attention and notoriety of the crimes that Manson, Dahmer and Gacy committed on the outside led to other inmates in the prison trying to claim the bragging rights on killing them.

Dahmer, who eventually became a born again Christian, made this statement to the court: "It is now over. This has never been a case of trying to get free. I didn't ever want freedom. Frankly, I wanted death for myself. This was a case to tell the world that I did what I did, but not for reasons of hate. I hated no one. I knew I was sick or evil or both. I know how much harm I have caused. Thank God there will be no more harm that I can do. I believe that only the Lord Jesus Christ can save me from my sins."

In the Columbia Correctional Institute in Portage, Wisconsin, Dahmer was eventually given janitorial work with Jesse Anderson and Christopher Scarver, a black schizophrenic who claimed to be the Son of God. This made the janitorial crew composed of three convicted killers. Picture how Scarver saw Jeffrey Dahmer, a man who had killed many black men and was now a born again Christian. It was a terrible mixture waiting to explode.

November 28, 1994. These three men began to do their work. Twenty minutes later, the guards came back to find Dahmer's head smashed and Anderson's lifeless body nearby. A bloody mop handle told the tale of Scarver's thoughts of the two men. Dahmer was pronounced dead at 9:11 a.m. Dahmer fell prey to one of the fame seeking, delusional inmates that morning.

No one can tell the stories better then those who live them out. They are the ones who see what we don't see and hear what we don't hear. They are the inmates of death row.

Maybe John Dillinger, the first man ever to be labeled "public enemy number one" by the FBI, said it best: "We can't all be saints."

"Methods of Execution"

There are six ways of leaving death row. One of these ways isn't easy to come by. The five most used ways to leave are by the use of lethal injection, electrocution, gas chamber, hanging and the firing squad. All of these draw to the same conclusion. The soul is sent out into eternity and the body is sent out of the prison yard in a coffin.

The not so easy way to leave is by being found innocent and being pardoned. Possibly even charged with a lesser crime and having the sentence dropped to life in prison or something less. Since 1976 not many of the inmates on death row have been so lucky as to leave the prison alive. As of February 8th, 2005, 948 have been executed in the United States. Since 1973, over 100 people in 22 states have been released from death row with evidence of their innocence. Florida leads the way with 21 and Illinois takes second place with 18 inmates taken off of death row. In the years 1999 and 2000 there were a total of eight inmates both years released from death row. This is possibly due to the new information that can be obtained through the use of DNA testing or various other modern ways of testing information.

The other five ways of leaving are:

Method 1 Lethal Injection:

Lethal Injection is the most common used means of execution in the United States of America. The condemned is secured on a gurney and receives several drugs intravenously. The inmate is secured with lined ankle, wrist and body restraints to the gurney in the preparation room outside the chamber. Cardiac monitor leads and a stethoscope are attached to the inmate. Two saline intravenous lines are injected one in each arm. The three chemicals used in the process are Sodium Thiopental, in a lethal dose that sedates the person and causes unconsciousness. Pancuronium Bromide, which is a muscle relaxant that collapses the diaphragm and lungs paralyzing them causing the inmate to stop breathing. And the final chemical injected is Potassium Chloride, the killer that stops heart. The inmate is covered with a sheet upon death.

Total cost of the execution runs about $86 for the cost of the chemicals. Lethal injection is seemingly the simplest and least painful method of execution.

The majority of the 38 states, which have the Death penalty, use this method. It is considered to be the most humane of the five ways to die.

Death usually occurs approximately seven to ten minutes after the lethal injection begins, according to the Texas Department of Criminal Justice.

Method 2 Electrocution:

The inmate's head is shaved so that the electrodes will make better contact with the body, then they are strapped to the electric chair. The electrodes are attached and the current is applied in varying amounts for two to three minutes. Electrocution produces visibly destructive effects as the internal organs of the inmate become burned.

The prisoner often jerks steadily against the restraining straps when the switch is thrown and the electrical current begins to flow throughout the soon to be corpse. The body changes to abnormal colors, the flesh swells, sometimes bursting from the pressure, and may even catch fire. In some instances sparks and flames are seen jumping from the inmate. The body temperature goes up to about 138 degrees Fahrenheit and is initially too hot to touch. Inner tissues are baked. The prisoner may defecate, urinate or vomit blood. The eyes may even be pushed from their sockets due to the extreme force of the electric flowing through the head. Witnesses always report that there is a smell of burning flesh.

Method 3 Gas Chamber:

The condemned prisoner is restrained in a chair inside a sealed steel chamber below which is a pan. Upon a signal, the executioner opens a valve, flowing hydrochloric acid into the pan. On a second signal, eight ounces of potassium cyanide crystals or sodium cyanide tablets are dropped mechanically into the acid, producing hydrocyanic gas. This gas destroys the hemoglobin in the blood, not allowing it to perform. Hemoglobin gives red blood cells their characteristic color and function primarily to carry oxygen from the lungs to the body tissues. Unconsciousness occurs within a few seconds. If the prisoner tries to hold their breath, the process can take much longer and can cause convulsions.

Death usually occurs within five to eighteen minutes. After pronouncement of death, the chamber is evacuated through carbon and neutralizing filters. Gas-masked crews decontaminate the body with bleach solutions and the body before being handled by an undertaker. An unsuspecting undertaker could be killed if this is not properly done.

Method 4 Hanging:

The death row inmate is weighed before the execution. A specific amount of force must be applied to the neck in relation to the weight of the inmate. If this is performed correctly, death is by dislocation of the third or fourth cervical vertebrae. This can cause over 1,000 pounds of force to the inmate's neck.

This is to assure almost instant death and neither strangulation nor beheading. The familiar noose coil is placed behind the inmates left ear, so it will snap the neck upon dropping. If not precisely executed, the inmate will strangle to death on the rope, die from lack of blood to the brain, or if dropped too far, decapitation can occur. This seems to be a painful and inhumane method of execution due to the potential for error.

Method 5 Firing Squad:

There is reportedly no set procedure, which according to information involves a five-man team, one of who will use a blank bullet so that none of them truly knows who was the real executioner. The team aims for the trunk of the body. Dependant on where the bullets hit is the time of death, which is relatively short.

"Where's Your Faith?"

The end of the road has come and death is knocking, these inmates have no choice but to let her in. These next few pages will show you the peace and tranquility of death or the brutality and scariness of entering an eternity not knowing what's next for your soul. What it all boils down to on your day of death is where you place your faith.

Many of them die in the execution chamber knowing their soul is saved and they are going to spend an eternity in Heaven with Jesus Christ. Others die trusting in something other than the blood of Jesus, which he shed on the cross for every human in this world. The difference can be seen in the compelling last words of these men. The difference can be seen in the attitudes and writings of these men. Not to say that the ones who claim to be saved individuals never sin, but there is a peace they have that is only given to men from God.

I am not here to judge anyone, but there is an obvious fact that is seen in some of these last statements. All of the men who are executed either speak of God and Jesus Christ before they go or they don't. It's a simple thing yet quite a profound thing. I am in no way saying that whoever doesn't speak or mention Jesus or God on their deathbed has a damned soul, which is lost and in danger of Hell. I am just summing up the facts of what is dwelling on their minds the last few minutes before they enter eternity.

The inmates, who died professing to be born-again Christians with saved souls, go out happy to enter Heavens kingdom and have a peace about their last words. On the other hand, the men who profess to not be saved or make no mention of it. These seem to have a more ruggedness and tenseness in the air in which their last words flow.

Can we really afford to turn them away? They were all at one time children and lived like regular people. Like us. Now they sit in the front row of a roller coaster ride of legal paperwork that all leads to their death. They belong to the system. Every day is the same to them. A tradition of waking up and basically doing the same thing they do every day on a set schedule. They seem to hang on to every word they write in their letters. Some choose to overlook God in their situation. Others bow to Jesus and worship Him. Some mix up bits and pieces of religion in a desperate hope to find what works to get them out. It all can be easily found in the Bible.

"In Their Own Words"

Michael McBride

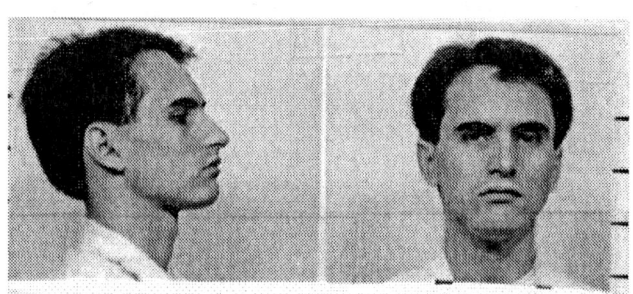

Source: www.tdcj.state.tx.us/index.htm 9/5/01

Michael Lee McBride entered the Texas Department of Corrections on May 26, 1988. Standing at 5'4" and weighing in at 141 pounds, McBride was to spend the next 12 years of his life, the last 12 years of his life, in a cell awaiting his death. This former bartender from California was convicted in the October 21st 1985 shooting deaths of Christian Fisher and James Alan Holzler, both 18-years-old from Lubbock, Texas. Fisher, McBrides ex-girlfriend and her companion were shot to death with a .30-caliber rifle, in a jealous rage, outside McBrides residence.

Witnesses said Fisher had gone to the residence to pick up some things and was killed by a hail of bullets after challenging McBride to shoot. McBride then walked to the victim's small Mazda and shot Holzler, who was seated in the driver's seat, in the head and the chest. Both died at the scene. McBride then turned the rifle on himself, shooting himself in the head, possibly by accident. Police found him lying on the ground and groping for the rifle.

May 11th 2000, McBride was 36 years old. His last meal consisted of two chicken patties with Swiss cheese. A stuffed baked potato with jalapeno peppers, sour cream and milk

That night he was pronounced dead at 6:21p.m. on the gurney where he received the lethal injection.

Michael McBride wrote this well-known poem out on his execution day as part of his last statement:

Do not stand at my grave and weep,
I am not there I do not sleep.
I am the diamond glints in the snow,
I am the sunlight on the ripened grain.
I am the gentle autumn rain.
When you awaken in the morning's hush,
I am the swift uplifting rush
Of quiet birds in circled flight,
I am the soft stars that shine at night.
Do not stand at my grave and cry,
I am not there. I did not die.
Signed
Michael L. McBride #903
May 11, 2000
Huntsville, Texas

The last statement of McBride:

Thank you, um, I anticipated that I would try to memorize and recite beatitudes New Testament, more or less, Luke's beatitudes, I should say, and a, a chapter on love in 1st Corinthians chapter 13, ah, I pretty much knew that I would not be able to memorize so much. There was also a poem that went along with it and in anticipation of not being able to, um, fulfill that desire, I provided a written statement that will be made available to anybody that wants it, I believe. Isn't that correct? So, uh, I wanted you to hear me say that and I apologize and for any other grief I have caused you know, including the, ah, what you're about to witness now. It won't be very long. As soon as you realize that appear I am falling asleep. I would leave because I won't be here after that point. I will be dead at that point. It's irreversible. God bless all of you. Thank you.

Source: www.tdcj.state.tx.us 9/5/01

Orion Joiner

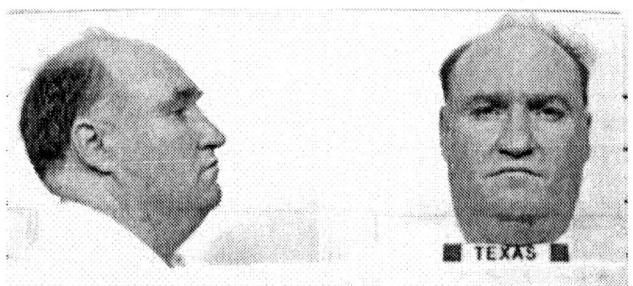

Source: www.tdcj.state.tx.us/index.htm 9/5/01

O.C. Joiner was a man who knew the meaning of peace on his day of death. He maintained saying he was innocent until his death. O.C. was found guilty in the December 1986 slayings of 26-year-old Lynette Huckabee and 29-year-old Eva Marie Deforest. Two waitresses who shared an apartment. Both were bound with duct tape inside the apartment and stabbed repeatedly. Huckabee, who was also raped, suffered multiple stab wounds to the chest, back and face and her throat was slashed. Deforest was beaten and stabbed 41 times and her throat was slashed. Joiner lived next door to the women and claimed he saw two black men running from the apartment after discovering their bodies. He was arrested after telling police conflicting stories about how he found the victims.

Source: www.tdcj.state.tx.us 9/5/01

Well Hello Mike,   6/21/00 6 p.m.

    Greeting In Christ Jesus. Thank so so much for thinking of me and writing to me but I have been saved now for about 20 years now. And I only have 17 more days before I get to go home to my Heavenly Father Jesus Christ. And Mike my friends call me O.C. or just Joiner. But it is ok if you call Orien to. And also Mike thank you for the books of John and Romans the one that I have already is so old and use that the pages are coming out of it. This will be the only letter you will get from me because I am so busy trying to get everything mailed out to my family before my execution and I have so much legal work to do for the execution date and everything and I'm also a member of lamp of Hope too and I have to get the last of my papers try up to mail out to. So I will close now and say goodnight and may God bless you and please keep up the good work and keep pass the Word of God out to everyone you can. I am proud to have known you and I will pray that your work in the Lord will stay well and safe.

Your Friend and Brother in Christ,   O.C.

Joiner's last meal:

A 1/2 lb. Hamburger steak (well done), brown gravy and grilled onions, large order of deep french-fried fries with ketchup, five pieces of buttered grilled Texas toast, iced tea with real sugar, hot honey buns with melted butter on the side.

Joiner's last statement:

Kathy, y'all take and I bless all of you and I am glad I have had y'all in my life. As I have said from the very first thing, I am innocent of this crime and God knows I am innocent and the people that was murdered know I am innocent and when I get to heaven I'll be hunting you and we'll talk. I feel sorry for the families that's had to suffer and my family and I have 'em all in my prayers. I love you all. Y'all take and y'all look after Sheila and Shannon and them, call 'em and get the pictures to 'em and everything and, ah, again, like I said, I feel sorry for the families, but if it takes my death to make them happy, then I will bless them. I have no hard feelings toward anyone cause the Lord feels that it is my time to come home to Him, my work on earth is done and that, ah, like I said, I am just sorry for, but they will have to go through this one time again, cause sooner or later, whoever did this crime is going to be caught and they'll have to come down here and do this again and they will realize they witnessed an innocent man going to be with Jesus Christ.

Source: www.tdcj.state.tx.us 9/5/01

Leo Little #999302

Source: www.tdcj.state.tx.us/index.htm 9/5/01

Summary of incident:
   On 01/25/1998, in San Antonio, Texas Little and co-defendant, Jose Zavalas, kidnapped a 22-year old Hispanic male and fatally shot him with a 25-caliber pistol during the commission of a robbery. The victim was kidnapped from a restaurant and died as a result from a single gunshot wound to the backside of his head. The victim had scratches and abrasions due to being dragged after he was shot.
   Source: www.tdcj.state.tx.us 9/5/01

Dear Mike,   August 28, 2001

    You may not remember me, but you had written me a letter back in January regarding my faith in God. I never forgot what you told me in that letter. I thought of your words often. Please allow me to explain why it took me all this time to write you back.
    When I received your letter, I sat on it. Meaning I didn't know what to do with it, so I didn't write back and I didn't throw it away. I wanted to at least write and say, "Thank you, but I am still struggling with my faith..." But about that time I was taken back to my hometown for something having to do with my appeals. So when I returned, I had a lot of things to sort out, and therefore I just couldn't write back and do that.

I never gave up on God. Or rather, God never gave up on me! He let me sort my problems out, and I know you'll be happy to hear, I accepted Jesus into my heart four days ago. August 24, 2001! I finally took that last step I've been holding back on. Whether that was God's plan or my own will power finally overcame Satan's grip on me...I don't know! But I know there's no turning back now. And I know this is only the beginning. I've committed myself to Christ, and I am not a person who forgets his word. I've waited so long to say those words... truthfully and with all my heart. It's going to be a hard road, but I think I'll make it. I know I will.

I just wanted to write and tell you the good news. Like I said, I never forgot what you said, and you asked me to tell you what I'd do. It took a little longer than both of us expected, but here I am. I'd really like your correspondence, your advice... and if you'd like to write back it would be most welcome. Perhaps we could become friends, you never know. Nevertheless, let me thank you for the time you took to write that letter you sent me. I'll never forget it. Thanks, and may God bless you and keep you safe.

Sincerely,
Leo

Mike,   June 4, 2002

Hey man, hopefully you are still at college, as its been a while since I had heard from you.

First off, I'm deeply sorry about not replying. Please forgive me. Although there's no good excuse, I should offer that I've been through much-spiritually and emotionally-but still I should have kept in touch.

This letter will be brief unfortunately, but I will write you a proper letter real soon. I'm writing you to see if the other brothers and sisters are around. I want to hear from you.

God bless you and give my love to the guys.
In Christ Jesus,
Leo

Dear Mike,   June 20, 2002

I pray my words reach you with much grace and blessedness. Peace be with you, your family and friends in the name of Christ Jesus.

I have never been the best letter writer, but now that God is with me, now that my faith is starting to make sense and solidify, you can expect that to change. I suppose the fellowship offer is still open?

Thanks a lot for the story you included last time, the one about the pardon. I must admit, I misunderstood it at first read, but of course when the spirit's with you it clears matters right up. Thanks again! I will definitely use it with some of the guys in here.

Along the same lines, there's this man at another prison that I am ministering to that doubt's God's existence. Now you know, a true believer would make a non-believer believe just by his attitude and outwardly appearance. But since we're not able to fellowship face to face, I had to take my time with his questions. His letter really took me a while, and Mike, I really hope he receives it well and puts his mistrust behind him. He's also homosexual, so there is an added roadblock for us to overcome. But I have faith! Pray for him will you? Adam is his name.

Hey man, tell me about yourself, like your daily life, family, friends, happenings. I'm real interested in getting to know you. And of course, any topic or questions you have coming my way are more than welcome.

I gotta go, but keep in touch and tell your roommates I have them in my prayers. God bless you Mike! Take care!
Psalm 112, In Christ Jesus,
Leo

Hey Mike,   July 10, 2002

I'm overjoyed that you got back to me. Thanks, I hope things are looking up for you. I have been keeping you in my prayers. Man, you sound busy. I'm telling you you're blessed, brother, to be able to accomplish some of the things you mentioned in your letter. I'm awestruck, may God bless you!

Now first, has Yates, Kevorkian or the Menendez brothers' written back? Definitely, I think one day, like me, they'll get their minds right, their souls in order, and get back to you. I was going through a ton of inner struggles (of which I won, glory to God) and it got ugly more times then I can count. But after the demons got tired of my resistance, they moved on, Amen! That's when I got back to you and began getting some things in order-which currently occupies most of my own time. They are in my prayers, I know exactly what some of them may be going through, I certainly do.

You're so lucky that you get to work with kids. Helping out like your doing has become my dream now-but only a dream.

However, I have been preparing to venture into that next level: reaching out. Most of it's in the infant and planning stages, like my willingness to teach some of the lost (actually my availability to it rather). I'm attempting to assemble coherent piece. Maybe a book addressed to parents, dealing with at risk, and troubled teenagers, giving my advice. I am also working on my autobiography. It is difficult because I am not a very good writer, but I am trying.

I'm also trying to come in contact with teenagers in tough positions. I'm doing that through juvenile judges and others' who are in that position to put that kind of trust in me. Maybe God doesn't quite think I'm ready for it, as I've had some setbacks and slowdowns, so I'll remain patient, as I should, and keep listening for the direction I should go. I believe he'll guide me to where I'm needed, and in that special way, I feel he has. I just need patience…

Well, you are in my prayers' and thanks again for writing. I'll be looking forward to hearing from you again. Love you, brother.

1st Samuel 3:10 "Speak; for thy servant heareth."

His and yours,
Leo

P.S. I turn 22 on the 14th so please pray that this year holds great things for me.

"For I through the law died to the law, that I might live to God. I have been crucified with Christ; it is no longer I who live, but Christ who lives in me; and the life I now live in the flesh I live by faith in the Son of God, who loved me and gave himself for me."
Galatians 2:19-20

-Livingston-9/20/02
Dear Mike,

Hey man, I was overjoyed to hear from you. I hope you are well, and that you are settled down now at school. Are you ready to tackle this semester, or no?

I'm heartened to hear that 7 of the kids in your youth group, that went to the Bill Rice Ranch got saved. Truly this is a blessing that has my heart singing God's praise…Glory to His name! Thanks for telling me that. I always love to hear of salvation, and of His will being carried out. It moves things enormous within me, and there's always a smile t be found upon my lips, and a gleam in my eye forms, for the Father's embrace is precious to behold; don't you agree?

I know what you mean, that you rededicated your life to God in all areas. I don't believe we'll ever stop evolving (growing in Christ). There's always that higher level of perfection that we humbly work for. We should take every opportunity that our Lord gives us to improve; and the worst thing one could do is sit idle and allow his faith to stagnate. The faith inside of us is alive! And it needs to be exercised, and fed and tested to mature and deepen. So I approve your 100% devotion...keep on my brother.

The last time Texas, at least south Texas where I'm from (San Antonio), has had snow was in 1986. I was 6 years old and I remember how slushie it was. None of that beautiful white stuff ya'll get up there. And that snow didn't stay long at all. But on the other hand, our summers last much longer. But be prepared to sweat.

It's been a hectic month around here. Two men I knew personally were executed back to back this week. It's saddening, but one of them was saved and so I can rest in that piece of comfort. Moreover I have been keeping myself highly busy lately. First and foremost I make worship prominent in my life. Reading and studying the Word takes up a lot of my days, praise Jesus. Hey, do you ever intend to pick up your Bible, intending on looking up something brief, do so, and then just, somehow get lost in its pages? Spending way more time than you intended? Isn't it awesome? I treasure His Word so much that I just eat and relish every word. I wish I could do nothing else but read his word, but unfortunately I have other, lesser responsibilities. I write many people from different countries...I'm learning French (and hopefully soon other tongues).

I'm occupied with three book right now. One on the aftermath of World War II in Europe (I'm a history nut). One on the IRA-it's history and characters and J.R.R. Tolkien's The Silmarillion. Haven't worked on the autobiography in a bit, but hopefully soon I'll be able to sit down and concentrate a bit. I'm thinking about switching up my sleeping schedule for that express purpose because it's way too noisy during the day around here. I'd also like to paint (watercolor) and that's a good nighttime activity that needs quiet. Though I hate sleeping during the day...I'm at a dilemma, but I'll work something out eventually. By selling paintings I will make, I want to fund a project I'm planning out to spread a little faith and happiness. Please pray for that, that I may find the time and success with it. It's definitely for the Father's glory, trust me :O) And I'm doing other things, this and that, you know…

Well, I'll let you go for now. I've got to write my own little "Joy" right now before she gets impatient and all worrisome. Her name's Mary, she's French and has awesome faith. I think I love her; known her almost two years, so you never know. I find true love takes a bit of time to see. So we'll see…

Peace be with you my friend; may the Lord bless you and keep you in His graces. Be well, brother, do good work and keep in touch. See ya…

Leo

1st Timothy 6:11-12
"But thou, O man of God, flee these things; and follow after righteousness, godliness, faith, love, patience, meekness. Fight the good fight of faith, lay hold on eternal life, whereunto thou art also called, and hast professed a good profession before many witnesses."

Dear Mike,   Oct. 4, 2002

Peace and the Lord's grace to you, my friend. As usual I am very happy to hear from you. I pray that everything is going well at MBBC.

First let me assure you that two of your prayer requests you mentioned have been part of my prayer life since you informed me, always, my friend. I have added your parents' plight as well as Josie's decision making. Anything else just holler.

So you used to write Calvin King? I never knew the man Rex either, but I personally, and the section of men that I'm housed with refuse the last meal trays and observe an hour (6-7) of silence each execution day in order to show our respects. To be honest with you, most do it just as defiance as if the guards realize (or care about) the reason for the silence and refusal. Regardless of their reasons I have mine and that's all that matters to me.

So how was it in Kenya? I imagine it being a very exciting adventure, going on a missions trip to Africa. How does all that work out? What methods do you use to minister to the natives'? I suppose you have an interpreter and that you help out established missionaries there already. It's not like village to village picking random people off the streets and preaching to them, is it?

I am glad that you want to do chaplain work in the future. I personally greatly appreciate my chaplains for the (sometimes) thankless job they dedicate themselves to. I let them know every chance there is that I feel this way. But, my friend, I ask you to not become discouraged when it seems like no one's listening, because they are, trust me. Just pray for the men you minister to and show them at all times the joy that Jesus has placed inside you and leave the heavy lifting to the Lord. I wish you luck! And if I am still with you I expect more joyful updates.

My so called painting is not yet fully formed as a hobby yet. For instance I've only done a half of a painting. Hey! I've been preoccupied lately! But hopefully I'll be able to exercise my creativeness soon. The half painting? Well since you asked about Mary, I'll go ahead and send you a picture of her that I'm using as a guide, but I've omitted her because I can't paint human forms even if I tried, and I could never do her justice.

Marie-Claire (Mary to me) turns 20 this February. I think I told you that she's French. She's got me wrapped around her finger, you know. She's brought much happiness into my life, and her faith in God is genuine and sure. She's young, and so am I, but we're in love. But It's a responsible love; the last thing I want is to mock the gift the Father has allowed us to experience. Lately her and I have been having really deep discussions about the proper place our feelings for each other should be, and how best to serve God in Christ with our love. It's interesting, this journey, that's for sure.

I met Mary through a friend. I had but one person to write at that time and he introduced us. We hit it off and it'll be three years since we met in December. I might give her my first painting since it is her house and cat I'm using as an example.

As far as if anyone in my family is saved, there are a few, but my closest loved ones are, I imagine, in limbo. Backsliders, and generally insincere when they tell me they're praying for me and of course I can never be entirely sure, but I know they don't talk about the Lord or comment when I do. You know how it is. I'm working on them though, and I implore you to do the same with your folks. You never know how the Lord will move them if you're persistent and patient with them. Also, try being heartfelt with your inquiries to their faith or lack there-of. I feel that prayer is the key to get the most stubborn of them all to stop being selfish and come to Jesus. If you speak from the heart with them, always respecting their choices I have faith they'll come around. I'll keep you posted about my family too.

So who is this Josie that I'm praying for? You say she is a new friend, what's she like? She's our age, you called her a kid?

She sounds lively, you pursuing? Oh don't mind my jokes, I'm just trying to assess the situation. I could imagine the nervousness you have when you're around her, but you seem like a great guy and I know if you really want her to take you seriously that you can make that happen. Just never change for anyone, but also, never refuse to grow for anyone either, and most importantly, I feel that if you show her that Christ lives inside you, and if you're patient, then God's will will be done regardless, and that's your (and my own) main focus in life. So don't worry about her for now, just be the best friend you know how to be.

Ok, on to your comments and questions. Nah, I'm not offended at all–I explain my past rather often. Yes, I'm afraid I did kill a man in cold blood. It's something that I wake up with and lay down with everyday, which out of respect for the man it's the least I could do to live with the shame. But, honestly, it's almost impossible to relate with that person I used to be. I used to angrily cry myself to sleep before I grew up; before my faith flourished into contentment and peace. Though I hold on to responsibility jealously, I look back at my act with detached disgust.

It was night, actually, I was 17 years old then. At the time I was using drugs heavily, drinking, and it's partly why I was fired from my job with a car payment due. I became desperate, looking for easy money so me and friend decided to rob someone. We robbed two people in similar patterns and the second time (which was rather greedy of us by the way) turned out totally different. I was intoxicated, with the man having knelt right in front of me on a pitch black, dark country road; with the emergency lights on his car blinking the only light out there; in the middle of winter, I shot the man, Christopher Antonio Chavez in the head for no reason at all. I was out of my mind, perhaps hallucinating, I don't really know. He was a Christian man, but that doesn't offer me or our families much consolation for such a loss. I heard at my trial that he was a really good man. I keep it in the back of my mind that maybe this was God's purpose. Something to think about, that's for sure.

About my picture, yeah I hate it too. I have hair now of course. That was taken at the end of a VERY long day, just arriving on death row. Shackles, transports, demeaning orders and body searches, and to top it off they sat me in a chair and shaved my head for a nice menacing mug shot for the papers later on. Pardon if it sounds bitter, but its true. Ever wonder why all those criminals look like they deserve what they got?

Oh, my days are as varied as they come. Most prominent are my studies of the Word of God, and letter writing, but other than those I'm still trying to strike a balance that works for me. There was a time when I had nothing to do but stare at the walls and fantasize about foolishness…

Which brings me to the "if I had 24 hours back in the free world" question. Do I have to make my way back to be on time, or is it like Cinderella, I lose the magic at midnight? Will I have notice of this wish, or plenty of time to have Mary with my family so that I can be with them, hug and kiss them and show them face to face the light of Christ in my eyes? Though that's selfish of me. I'd have a hard time choosing that or pleading with Christopher's family for forgiveness (but that remains a possible reality though, unlike the former example).

Here, I have some people who act like friends to me. What I mean is that I consider everyone a friend, but there a few that I prefer there company to others. Talking about vulgar and immoral subjects aren't my cup of tea, so I mainly stick to myself, really. I hardly talk, other than to myself when I practice my languages, singing and reading aloud. Sometimes I just have to randomly speak to let myself know I'm still present! I know my neighbors enjoy that I'm their neighbor because I don't act like a fool like a lot of people do, being just plain obnoxious. But to each his own, no amount of ignorance will ever trap me in sin again. Read Jude 17-23; Col. 4:5-6 and Titus 3:1-7 for my attitude towards them.

Do me a favor and send me a picture of you and Josie, I like to know who I'm praying for…nah, really I just like pictures. Take good care of yourself brother, and stay in the Word.

Jesus is Lord,
Leo

Leon Lawrence
(The name of this inmate, and locations, were changed to protect the innocent)

Date of Birth: 1973
Prior Prison Record-None
Summary of incident:
    Lawrence shot and killed a male during a drug deal. Two other male victims were also shot during the incident. Lawrence drove another victim, a black female to an abandoned house and shot and killed her. Her body was discovered two days later.

Dear Mike,   1-30-01
    Greetings and love always in the name of our Lord and Savior Christ Jesus! Psalm 20:6-8 "Some trust in chariots, and some in horses: but we will remember the name of the LORD our God. They are brought down and fallen: but we are risen, and stand upright. Save, LORD: let the king hear us when we call."
    I must tell you that it is a pleasure to have heard from you, a brother in Christ, my family! I received your letter on 1-26-01 and I shall respond. My name is Leon Lawrence. I am 26 years old, father to two girls. I am from Florida and I've been in prison for two years now, one year on the row. I AM INNOCENT, of any crime, I just got caught up in politics and poverty. I am also the oldest of my five siblings.
    You asked me where would I go if I were to die? Heaven or Hell? Well, Acts 2:21 "And it shall come to pass, that whosoever shall call on the name of the Lord shall be saved." Well I called on Christ's name on 2-16-99. Therefore I will expect to be in Heaven, among the other believers.
    I must admit that shortly before 2-16-99 I knew little to nothing about Jesus Christ and any belief in a Supreme Being (God) was always up for debate. I am not proud of my old nature, however it is my old nature. See I used to live a life of drugs, adultery, lies etc… Since the age of 16 years old, though I didn't like that life, at first. I began to become that which I hated. I wanted to be a cop growing up. I lived in a small three-bedroom house (shack), with three families (12 people). Growing up wasn't that hard for me, cause I didn't have any responsibilities. My mom worked three jobs six days a week and life was hard for her. I fell in

love with basketball. I played and practiced from 6a.m. until 8p.m. at the age of 15 years old. I had a basketball scholarship to a junior college in Mississippi, but I would have played my last year in school, major colleges would have picked me up.

Wanting things that my eyes seen caused me to fall into a deep depression cause I couldn't have the material stuff of the world. I fell in love with an older girl who became pregnant. I had pressure from her to provide for our upcoming child. My dad had walked out on my mom and us when I was five years old, so 10 years later he appears again. This time he gives me drugs to sell. I used to think drugs was evil then, cause of all the warnings our teachers and officers gave us. But here was my dad, though he never was here for me, I still loved him. I changed the way I though, figuring if dad says its ok, its ok! Anyways the rest is history. I became my worst enemy, a drug dealer. In fact, I was the biggest drug dealer in parts of Florida. Therefore it is no secret I am on Death Row for a drug-related offense. It's ironic, but sad to me!

I was arrested in 1998, but I was mad, my heart was twice as hard as pharaoh's heart. God, Jesus and being saved was the last thing on my mind. But, every letter I got talked about Jesus. Every prison cell I went in had Christian brothers who sung day and night about Christ. I witnessed hopeless men cry tears of repentance. I seen men hug each other and hold hands, something that was strange to me. I seen men, who the DA and other lawyers said wouldn't go home, within days to us humans and seconds to God, they went home. Indeed I became curious, but I was still depending on myself and other men, not God. In Jan. of 99 I was charged with another capital murder (making it 2). I decided to attempt to know God and Christ. I began to attend church meetings in the jail, read my Bible and pray. I started to believe. I prayed for others and I seen my prayers answered. It was amazing. But I still had a lot of anger, rage, hate etc… inside of me. It wasn't until Feb of 99 when I was moved to another jail and charged with another capital murder (making it 3). My life in the eyes of others was over. I got closer to Christ. Men who couldn't read or write would bring me Christian material to read for them. In return I learned more and explained to others what I learned. I never been in any jail, prison or any criminal institute before. But in between the months of Dec. 98-July 99 I had been in 2 county jails, 2 penitentiaries in LA and in 1 county jail in Houston. All, I mean all were a spiritual growth experience. For I was always around brothers in Christ. June 99, my trial was about to begin and my lawyers assured me that I would go home. Some of the charges were dropped against me. So in a prodigal son kinda way, I turned once again against God and back to man. I hadn't learned to trust in God and believe on His promises. Anyway, I was convicted! Do I blame God? No! Do I blame myself? No! Job taught me not to blame, just be patient.

And that's where I am now. It's hard at times to be patient, but I know that after hard patience comes the satisfaction of rest. Had it not been for Jesus, I would not be writing you now nor would I be sane mentally and perhaps I might not be alive. But I am and so I give praise to God my Heavenly Father and I thank Jesus for being my Savior, my Redeemer, my Friend and go to when I am down and out.

So all I could tell God if he asked me is thank you Father God for allowing Jesus to cleanse this sinner and making me a child of God.

So, there you have a short view of my life, my faith and my beliefs. Yes, I ask God to have mercy on me and to give me another chance at freedom. But I am sure God wont leave me, so whatever His will is. God knows what I go through here. It is far away from being peaches-n-cream. Staying in a small 9'x6' cell, 24 hours a day, alone, can take its toll. Job 13:16 "He also shall be my salvation: for an hypocrite shall not come before him."

So, tell me about yourself? What are you taking up in college? Do you have any family? Sorry that the New York Giants didn't win!

But I must encourage you to continue reaching out and to spread our Lords words. You are indeed a disciple. I must let it be known you are my family, my bro and we will meet. Maybe in the flesh (this world), but definitely in Heaven Amen.

Sincerely Your Bro. Lawrence

Dear Mike, 3/28/01

PSALM chapter 119 v 50 "This is my comfort in my affliction: for thy word hath quickened me." AMEN

It was and always will be a blessing to hear from you: and I pray that you continue to live a life as a servant; Doing what "GOD" wants us to do. We all must witness to others; mainly the unsaved. It is our duty!

You know I am blessed and so are you and the many others. I am sure I mean ALOT to many people; but I had to endure pain; I was a "prodigal son" who had to be corrected; in order to be a child who honored my Heavenly Father! But I'll be truthful to you, "I ADMIRE THE CHILD THAT NEEDS NO CORRECTION!" Like you and the many others who believe from jump!

I've missed out from early on, and my shame (guilt) is always before me; but now I have gained the most important thing ever, my salvation! Yes, I'm late but I'm here.

Well it's just another day here; a day of many negative things; but a day to be thankful and THANK GOD! Cause my (GOD) didn't have to wake US UP! And on that note, Paul gave life meaning (Philippians 1 v 22) "But if I live in the flesh, this is the fruit of my labour: yet what I shall choose I wot not."

Yes, one day we shall meet in Heaven; but my life does not rest there. My "faith" says I shall be free from this place. Man says it's impossible and the ODDS are AGAINST ME! But I choose to believe in the creator not the creation. History is made on any given day. And any day history can and will be made. I don't know "HOW" or "WHEN", but I do know "WHO"! That being our HEAVENLY FATHER!

I HAD three murder charges. Two were dismissed and I also believe this murder charge will be dismissed also.

Each tragedy in life has a meaning; more powerful then just crying or feeling self-pity or asking why? To loose is to gain, if you believe! Job believed and he gained, after he lost. In fact; starting with Abraham and ending in Rev. with John, all, lost but gained (Ephesians 3:20) God is able to do more then I could ever ask for or imagine. And I'm sorry to report, but many claim to believe in God and they may; but they don't believe in "GOD ALMIGHTY"! Cause to believe is also to believe in something..."A PROMISE", the same promise that God gives everyone (MATT. 21:22) "And all things, whatsoever ye shall ask in prayer, believing, ye shall receive."

What makes a great ball player? The fact that he believes. What made Bill Gates a computer whiz? The fact that he believed. Now whether or not they believe in God is another subject, but faith plus belief equals achieving or as I call it making history; beating the odds.

Of course my faith needed a direction, cause my HOPE was shot after my conviction. I needed help, and just like Gideon; the Lord heard and answered my prayers (Judges 6:17). Gideon replied that if you are pleased with me, give me a special sign, then I'll know its really you talking to me! So the Lord has built my faith on many things that let me know He is watching over me! There are ALOT of things wrong in my case. Things that no one can explain. When things can't be explained by MAN, then you can only believe, GOD DID IT! I'll share one of my most favorite scriptures in the bible; although there are 31,173 verses in 66 books of the Bible; ONE REALLY, REALLY MOTIVATES ME: (Mark

9:23- 24) " Jesus said unto him, If thou canst believe, all things are possible to him that believeth. And straightway the father of the child cried out, and said with tears, Lord, I believe; help thou mine unbelief."

Simply, Jesus give me what I need; cause I'm trying. If I don't believe, make me believe! If I doubt take away my doubt and fears etc...

Well I'm glad to hear that you are in school and you are seeking your degree. In the world "EDUCATION" is a major plus. So I encourage you to go forward; everyday learn and share your knowledge I will pray for your family; as I do for all unsaved persons or families you must continue to stand on your belief and by prayer; maybe God will soften their hearts and maybe salvation in truth will be accepted.

I'm not a hockey guy, but we share a common interest in basketball. I also am a fan of Camby; but, I know I can beat him one on one I used to be real good, I had a college scholarship from other schools, just made a bad choice in life. I'm out of shape now. I'm still quicker then the average, but I know I've lost a step or two I barely can dunk now. In my prime; I was a human dunk show! It's been over a year since I played a game of b-ball. So I know I'm washed up. Before my arrest, I played ball for a semi-pro city league and most of our opponents were ex-college stars or almosts (like myself), I can play any position, I love the physical play; I even found myself playing against guys who were 6'7" or taller. I would shut them down! I'm only 5'11" or 6'0". When I got a good pair of Jordan's. But that was then. Now my small cell is my court, Which I am trapped in this cell for 24 hours. A day (not good). But I do love the game and I have made a paper goal, and a paper ball, add a little imagination and well "THE BIG LIGHTS ARE ON ME AGAIN," even thou its only a figment of my imagination, anyway...

I'm glad to hear about brother Jared, the Lord is really using you two. Build each other up; encourage others. And when time gets rough, pray that God make you tougher.

I'll send you a picture of me; hopefully my mom will make copies. Anyway (Romans 1:7) "To all that be in Rome, beloved of God, called to be saints: Grace to you and peace from God our Father, and the Lord Jesus Christ."

Dear Mike,

Greetings and love always. 1ˢᵗ Timothy 4:13 "Till I come, give attendance to reading, to exhortation, to doctrine."

Hello, my brother! It is good as always to hear from a member of Christ's family! Just so you know, your education is the key! If I hear from you in one week or one year; does not bother me. Knowing you are trying to better yourself for adulthood in this world and better yourself in the nest (Heaven); is what I am concerned about.

I may not be with you in body; but I am joined with you in spirit! 1ˢᵗ Corinthians 5:4 "In the name of our Lord Jesus Christ, when ye are gathered together, and my spirit, with the power of our Lord Jesus Christ."

So I hope and pray that your tests were passive, and the work load was lifted off your shoulders.

Allow me to briefly explain something to you, Mail is the most sought after message a prisoner seeks. It's the main contacts to others; especially here on DEATH ROW! We have no television, no group recreation; no anything; besides mail! Therefore mail becomes a personal addiction from one person to another!

There are some things that others would say that isn't nor wasn't supposed to come out (feel me). Many will call themselves believers to gain the sympathy of true Christians who have soft compassionate hearts. They (some prisoners) will try to use the "free world people" and claim Christianity. So they aren't believers, they are users (non-believers). But I feel if you deal with a individual on a set level, he/she can become a "true believer" through our or other testimonies.

You have "No IDEA" the evil sprits that lives in a prison unless you have been apart of a prison system; and believe me, the forces here are "VERY DECEIVING"!

As far as myself! Well, I have my ups and downs, but I'm blessed regardless!

In order for one to really appreciate a BLESSING; One must know the experience of suffering! So, when that blessing comes, it will be a reminder that suffering do have its satisfying joy in the end...if we suffer for Christ.

You asked me "If I was sure my murder charges would be dismissed?" You know I'm not sure of much, besides GOD IS FAITHFUL and TRUE; even though we (sinners) aren't FAITHFUL and TRUE! I just know I shall be set free again, I don't know when, how or whether it's dismissed or a deal is made; I just know I'm going home.

Lawyers told me before I was convicted, that I would never be found guilty; but here I am ISAIAH 2:22 "Cease ye from man, whose breath is in his nostrils: for wherein is he to be accounted of?"

A true Christian lives by faith HEBREWS 11:6 "But without faith it is impossible to please him: for he that cometh to God must believe that he is, and that he is a rewarder of them that diligently seek him."

When I was a non-believer I had NO FAITH and like the world, I BELIEVED IN ONLY WHAT I COULD SEE. Now I'm a Christian, through my suffering and bondage; and I have faith and believe in things I can not see. Cause many of my prayers were "BLIND" and yet "GOD" answered them and gave me spiritual sight! AMEN! Peter believed and walked on water, Moses believed and parted a whole sea, Daniel believed and slept among lions, Saul believed and was converted to Paul and etc...you or me (all believers) can do the same.

Dear Mike,   Greeting and grace forever.

Daniel 10:13 "but, lo, Michael, one of the chief princes, came to help me"

Indeed we are brothers, joined together by our Lord and savior Jesus Christ!

MATTHEW 17:27) "Notwithstanding, lest we should offend them, go thou to the sea, and cast an hook, and take up the fish that first cometh up; and when thou hast opened his mouth, thou shalt find a piece of money: that take, and give unto them for me and thee." I'm sure that if you ask the Lord, he will find a way to get the 500 dollars you are missing to get to Africa. I hear Africa is a beautiful place and by any chance you do go, remember to take a camera, and take a few pictures for me please. I would love to see the scenery.

I wanted to tell or ask you last time. Was that a picture of the Christian college, where you attend? If so, man that place seems to be "BEAUTY OF A PORTRAIT!" A MONA LISA OF BUILDINGS.

Yes I still have my four gold teeth. I put them in back in 1993. In fact; most of my family have gold in their mouth. Now more then ever, When I put mine (back in the days) it was only a few of us and our gold gave us away. The teeth was the witness against us and our drug dealing in the street.

You asked me what it is that I miss the most? Well I would say, I

MISS MY FREEDOM THE MOST! The will to go shopping, go to the mall and spend the whole day in the arcade room, to take long hot tub baths with cologne or bath beads. The smiling faces of my kids, the warmth from my mom, family and close friends.

For 23 years of my life (I'm 26 now) I have been independent, a lover of other gods (Women, cars, gold, money etc...) One who had "HIGH RESPECTS" from others; like a movie star. So sure, I miss or lust for a few worldly things. However I do pray on my weaknesses. Rome wasn't built in a day and NO NEED FOR ME TO FOOL MYSELF and think I can be changed in a day. 2nd Corinthians 4:16 "For which cause we faint not; but though our outward man perish, yet the inward man is renewed day by day." Our bodies will suffer, but our spirit is getting stronger. So, as Paul mentioned, the battle is an ongoing struggle. We are in the flesh and as long as we are, we shall suffer in the flesh. I don't want to sin. But I can and will be molded into an image of perfection and so will you.

If I had 24 hours? Man! You know I'm not scared of death, never was. I believe I was scared of the way I would die. I was scared of fire! And had a fear of dying in a house fire.

Its funny, well more less ironic you asked this question, cause I have asked myself this exact question countless times. Well when I got arrested, it came at a time that I had made many family members mad at me or we where mad at each other. I left when my oldest child was five, the others were around a year to a year and a half. But there are two little girls that I have not seen or touched. So my first twelve hours, would be spent in my mom's arms, as well as my kids. Let them know I will always love them. Try to get my kids to know that "EDUCATION" is the key to the way out (poor living). My mom is one of the best moms God ever created. I'm not saying that cause she is my mom, but hey, she is a strong mother, single parent and leader and Christian who loves her enemies more then herself.

My next 4 hours, would be playing basketball, my true love and passion! I want the best to play against.

The next 2 hours would be at my favorite restaurant, Indulging in my favorite foods, such as gumbo, fish, etc...

For my final 6 hours, I would want to spend it in an empty beautiful park: Me alone! There I would enjoy the peace of self and of nature. I would meditate to GOD; repent of any or all sins and talk to myself. After that, everything is MEANINGLESS; unless God gives me something, by sending me off on a mission. The fact is life or death would not even bother me from that point on.

So, I hope I have at least gave you at least a step or two, to what you were wanting to know.

On a sadder note...my step mom was brutally murdered and hog tied in her home on 4-20-01, I'm ok; but I was devastated. So I ask for your prayers, prayers for healing toward me and my family. Until next time my dear friend/ brother

1st Thess. 5:28 "The grace of our Lord Jesus Christ be with you. Amen"

Dear Mike,   5-29-01

Greetings. Psalms 18:28 "For thou wilt light my candle: the LORD my God will enlighten my darkness." Good day and good blessings be upon you and your family today, tomorrow and the days to come. I am as well as one can expect. I thank God daily for strength and I thank Jesus for peace and love I receive in my times of tribulation and trouble. It's rough living in solitary confinement. One must have faith to truly make it. My faith may be small but I do have faith in God. I know if I stay joined to Christ he will stay by me.

The U.S.A. is a sinful nation and crime will only get worse. We teach, by way or radio and TV, kids from a young age to kill. The rich kill too but they pay their way out. The poor kill and are made out to be pure evil, not worthy to live. If anyone feels that is justice then they are as evil as the ones who killed Jesus Christ.

My step-mom is dearly missed already. She was so young and didn't have to die in that horrible way. There are no suspects and the neighbor's claim that they heard nothing. No one seen anything and this happened on an early Friday evening, in a very high security area. I haven't heard from my dad since then. My aunt wrote me and last I heard the family was still traumatized. There is a lot of cry and questions about why it happened. It hit me like an 8.0 earthquake for about four days. But now there is nothing I could of done to prevent it and nothing I can do to comfort anyone since I am in here. That's the downside to being locked up. Death comes to the young and the old. Natural deaths and tragic deaths happen at random.

Mike, I was once one of the most powerful men in my game. Whatever I said was done. I had an army at my use. I had respect from young and old alike. So much money, I spent at least $1,000 on an average day. I gambled heavy and once lost $10,000 in 4 hours. I had my choice of any cars that wanted between 96-98. No one ever spoke loudly to me in fear of me. I always had dreams of making it big. I was a young, fighting thug back then. I lived to fight and faced death many times. I have been kidnapped, beaten and robbed many times. Then my break came in 1995. I met this guy and he would front me dope. One day he fronted me $18,000 worth of drugs and when I went to pay him, I found out the Feds had busted him. So the $18,000 was mine and the rest is drug history. From being a thug in jeans to mature respectable man in suits. Then in one fatal moment, all I once had was gone. Five seconds was all it took. I was wrongly accused and wrongly convicted and wrongly robbed out of my life.

Saying that, that's why I put my family and their problems in a box. If I didn't then I'd be more miserable then ever. The Bible lifts me up and it's the only thing. Many people compare themselves to Job, Paul etc…that's fine! I relate to them too. I am more like King Nebuchadnezzar. Being a king brings a kingdom and I once had a kingdom. Like Nebuchadnezzar I lost it all and live like an animal. Here on (Satan's Den) Death Row.

I have lost many family members and loyal friends since I have been here. They along with their memories are in that box! My step-mom was duct-taped from her feet, hands and mouth. She was beaten in a way someone gets beast for information, lots of damage to her face and mouth. 90% of my family do what I used to do. It is the family business sad to say. We were raised that way and even I didn't think it was wrong until now. Now my fear is for my kids and their upbringing. The chain must be broken. For to many I am a hero, so no one learns from my experience, instead they follow the same wrong path. And I am helpless! I tell them about my belief in God and I tell them to change. My words to them only float like the wind, never resting on the heart. They think I am only Christian cause I am in jail. Bottom line, for the first time in my life, I'm helpless.

No where in the Bible does it ever say that being saved is trouble free. We must give the people the whole truth. We suffer cause Christ suffered for us sinners. One day our endurance through our suffering will make us approved in Christ's eyes.

Well, I must end for now but my thoughts and prayers are with you. Continue to practice your jump shot. Practice may not make you perfect but it will make you better for tomorrow. Perhaps if I ever get out and we meet in this world I can show you some of my moves instead of telling you.

    Keep the faith and love,
        Sincerely your brother in Christ, Leon

Pam Perillo

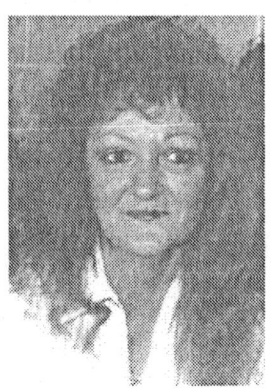

To Whom Ever It May Concern: 4-21-99

My name is Pamela Perillo, I'm a Death Row inmate in the State of Texas. I have been on Death Row since Sept. 5th, 1980, almost 19 years.

There are only 8 of us females on Death Row in Texas, three of us are non-work capable by choice and two others were put on a administrative segregation status because the Medical Department said they couldn't pull cotton (repetitive work) because of carpal tunnel syndrome. We are being treated like animals right now just because we are Death Row inmates. We have been placed in a small cell behind a solid door, we get "one" hour recreation per day. They schedule that so early in the morning that no one wants to go. We also only get one hour of TV five days a week. The male Death Row inmates have TV's outside their cells all down the run, and get it turned on from 7:00 am until 11:00 pm through the week. On weekends their T.V. viewing time is 7:OO am until 1:30 am. Not only do the women not get to view T.V. during the same hours we don't even have any.

We are also being strip searched six, some times eight times a day, and most of the time we have never left our cells from one search to another. They go through our property with no care what-so-ever in the way they handle it. Our property is left all over our cells when they are done searching. My lock box was closed on my picture of my daughter who died, she was in her coffin and they put a big hole in her head. When I showed it to the Lt. she said "What do you want me to do about it?".

They have all five of us who don't work living in a building they call the Multi-purpose facility, they house crisis management psychiatric

patients, seg. inmates, and Death Row non-work capable inmates all in this building. "These women in crisis management are brought in here at all times of the day and night in various stages of hysteria, fear, or anger, a lot of them come in cut up from attempted suicides. These women are subjected to gassings with pepper spray for different reasons which instantly affects everyone around the area especially as no windows open in this building. We have witnessed numerous women who are most obviously out of their senses have excessive uses of force applied. Such as slamming them to the floor and against the walls. We have heard officers sit around laughing and making fun of these women which have honest mental diseases. I heard one officer say "We had to spray that nut three times, she just sat there batting that pepper spray up." It's really sad to see and hear the way they are treated in here. A female inmate died in here not long ago. She was brought over here from another unit right after a use of force was done on her at the unit she came from. She came over here on a Friday to the crisis management part of this
building, very hurt and sick. Because it was a weekend there was no Dr. on the unit and none called in to see her.

They had one officer working that Friday night on 3rd shift, at 3:00 am. When the officer looked in on this woman she was covered in feces black as tar, which means it had blood in it, and no one would clean this lady up because there was only one officer here. She sat in that cell all weekend with blood and fluids coming out every hole in her body. When Monday came the Dr. who is actually a PA wouldn't see her and she died that Wednesday. Of course TDCJ finds a scapegoat for everything that happens so they fired two nurses and one Dr. I have seen many inmates suffer because of a lack of proper medical care here.

The female Death Row work capable inmates work 7 1/2 hours a day pulling cotton apart and one SSI job. For their 7 1/2 hours of work they only receive two hours of rec. a day, no T.V.'s down their runs at all. We have been separated from general population because we are Death Row inmates not because we are bad actors, yet we are treated like we are.

When they take a Death Row inmate to the visiting room they lock the inmate in a cage. The transport officer leaves the building with the keys. They actually leave the inmate, one officer and the visitors in the locked building with no way to escape in case of a fire.

We are being cuffed and put in a day room with cuffs on and left alone when they are searching our cells. We have no way of helping ourselves if something happens. There has never been any violence on the female Death Row in all the years I've been here.

We are in these little cells all day long just because we are on Death Row, with no T.V. and no room to move around. We don't even have a stool and table in here to eat or write on. We have to eat our meals on our bed, floor or toilet. They came in here the other day and covered up one of the outlets in our cells, so now we only have one outlet to use for all our electrical appliances. (Radio, fan, typewriter, hot pot, curling iron, blow dryer etc.)

The school was able to bring over newspapers and magazines for us to read but the Warden said Death Row inmates couldn't read them anymore, but population inmates still can.

Death Row inmates states are to be separated from general population they say to maintain safety, security and order amongst general population offenders and correctional personnel. But we are all Death Row inmates right here together for years, and they are telling us we can't talk to each other. They want us to sit here behind a solid door 24 hours a day for years, alone, and not talk to anyone?

What happened to the Death Row Activity plan that was the David Ruiz Civil Action # H78987? Are these people no longer under this court order? Every time we turn around they are taking something else away from us. If you can't help us can you refer this letter to someone who can? I would very much appreciate it if you could give me a yes or no answer on whether or not we are still under the Ruiz Death Row Activity Plan?

Thank you so much for your time, patience, and assistance.
Sincerely,
Pamela Lynn Perillo   TDC # 000665

Clay Smith

In Pine Bluff, Clay King Smith was sentenced to die by lethal injection after a jury found him guilty Thursday of five counts of capital murder.

Outside the courtroom, Brenda Cox Bratton, the mother of victim Samantha Rhodes, told reporters, "He may have sent my daughter to heaven, but today the state sent him to hell."

Bratton was referring to testimony Wednesday in which Jay Moser, an investigator with the Jefferson County sheriff's office, said Smith told him during a standoff with officers that "I sent three of them to Heaven. I don't know where in the hell the other two went."

It took the jury of eight women and four men about an hour to decide the fate of Smith, 28. The trial lasted four days at the Jefferson County Courthouse. Relatives of the victims wept openly as Circuit Court Judge H.A. Taylor read the sentence. Extra deputies packed the courtroom Thursday to prevent outbursts and to keep order.

Last year, Smith was charged in the March 25, 1998, deaths of his girlfriend, Misty Erwin, 20, who lived with him in a mobile home near Jefferson; Erwin's cousin, Shelly Sorg, 24, of Pine Bluff; Sorg's children, Taylor Nicole Sorg, 3, and Sean Michael Sorg, 5; and family friend Samantha, 12, also of Pine Bluff.

Deputies found the victims in Smith's two-bedroom home after relatives filed missing person's reports with the sheriff's office. All of the victims had been shot multiple times in the head except for Taylor Sorg, who was killed by a single gunshot wound in the face, an expert from the state Crime Laboratory in Little Rock testified Wednesday.

Walt Chavis, an El Dorado police officer and Smith's brother, was brought to the scene to talk Smith into surrendering. After the verdict Thursday, Chavis said, "it hasn't been easy. It's just something you have to bear." Smith is the youngest of six brothers, Chavis said.

During closing remarks, Deputy Prosecuting Attorney Kim Bridgforth said, "There is nothing more deliberate than when you walk up to a 5-year-old child and shoot him in the head."

Smith's attorney, Dale Adams of Little Rock, pointed to "gaps in evidence, the fact that cigarette butts, a whiskey bottle and blood splatters on the walls and ceiling and a fingerprint at the front door were not sent to the crime lab for analysis.

"They zoomed in on him and didn't consider anybody else," Adams said, adding that Shelly Sorg's husband, who had threatened her three times, "was never eliminated as a suspect."

Adams said if jurors had reasonable doubt, they could opt for a lesser sentence of 1st or 2nd degree murder or acquittal.

On Thursday morning, Adams and Smith's other attorney, Maxie Kizer of Pine Bluff, began the day by resting their case without calling a single witness after Smith declared that he wanted to serve as his own attorney.

The jury went out at 11:10 a.m. to deliberate Smith's guilt or innocence. While they were out, Smith's attorneys announced that Smith did not want them to introduce any mitigating circumstances during the penalty phase of the trial.

Taylor asked Smith if he knew he had a constitutional right to offer such evidence to the jury. He also asked Smith if he was under the influence of any drug, alcohol or had a mental disease that would prompt him to make such a decision.

"Do you realize the consequences?" Taylor asked.

"Yes," Smith responded.

"Do you want to share with the court why you are doing this?"

"No," Smith responded.

Kizer then summarized the evidence he said he would have presented if Smith had let him, which included the fact that Smith had no significant criminal history and had attended Central Bible College in Springfield, Mo., for three years.

He said Smith had become a youth minister but had had recurring drug problems since he was 12 years old.

The jury returned about 12:30 p.m. and delivered their guilty verdict on all five counts.

When the jurors returned from lunch at 2 p.m. to begin deliberating the penalty phase, Taylor told them of Smith's decision. Smith then stood before them and made a rambling statement.

Smith said. "You've accused me of killing the most loved person in my life, my fiancée (Misty Erwin). While I may not agree with the jury's verdict, you must respect it."

Prosecuting Attorney Steve Dalrymple objected, and Taylor admonished Smith to confine his comments to the penalty phase of the trial.

Smith said he had played with one of the child victims and also tried to get the prosecutors to project a photograph of Misty Erwin onto a monitor for the jurors, which drew another objection from Dalrymple.

After a short conference between the attorneys, Smith stood back up and told the jury, "I respect your decision. You found me guilty of killing Misty and four other people. I've lost my life anyway."

Dalrymple told the jury that Smith "still stands in denial. There are no mitigating circumstances. The state has asked for the Death penalty, and we do not do that lightly."

The jury went back out at 2:59 p.m. to deliberate Smith's sentence. Jurors returned about 4 p.m. with a recommendation that he be put to death.
(Arkansas Democrat-Gazette, Newspaper 1998)

Michael   6-5-00

I appreciate your efforts brother in reaching out to the Death Row population. Well I'm saved and the Lord has brought me a long ways from where I was. It's a really long story but I am going to send you a short version of my testimony and maybe some other stuff I've written. I write a lot of people and try to encourage them in the Lord and vice versa.

For as long as I have been saved the thought of Heaven has made me long to depart this life and be with Jesus. I know this mortal will put on immortality and this weakness will put on power, this corruptible will put on incorruptible, when we see Jesus we will be like Him. No more sinful nature that we inherited from Adam. No this corruptible will put on incorruptible- we will have a divine nature. No more struggle with sin. Praise God. I also have had a lot of hard times in this life. It's been tuff tuff. I've fought depression hundreds of times. Sure I've leaned on the Lord and cried out to him and just by grace he has brought me through. I screw up a lot but like a good soldier I get backup and ask the Lord to brush me off and make me clean again and then move on. Proverbs 24:16 "For a just man falleth seven times, and riseth up again: but the wicked shall fall into mischief." I know you mean well brother but you didn't get woke up by the stench of poo poo cause somebody threw a turd in front of your cell door or hear someone screaming all night. Sounds terrible and I am not even telling the bulk of it. The Lord is my strength and shield, my high tower and my refuge. He does give me peace that surpasses all understanding and strength to endure but I am in a battle. We don't quit even when it hurts, do we brother. We grit and bare it. These trials just make us stronger in Him. We lean on Him that much more.

I did some work up in New York one time. I was a welder. I lived at Scroon Lake and worked at a shut down paper mill in Ticonderoga. I remember Sabbath Point was near a bunch of little towns. Real nice people. Very beautiful. I passed like five lakes in 20 miles on the way to work. It was nice. Should have tried to stay. Well man I hope you write me back. Say what you feel; I need all the prayer I can get. I need Gods anointing to help me to write and proclaim the Word. I am going to stick some sermons in here, use them if you want. I need your prayers brother. Remember me.

  Clay Smith

Mike   7-2-00

  I like your abstract poetry or whatever it's called. That's pretty cool. I hope things work out for you with finding someone to spend your life with. I probably wouldn't be here if I had at the right time but don't ever get mad at God and rebel. That's what I did. I should have been patient and just hung in there and I know things would have worked out.

  I had a girl I was in love with for several years. She was in 11th grade and I was starting college. When she graduated I thought it was ok to ask her out now. About five minutes before I did someone else did and they started going out and got engaged. I backslid about this time. I'd had a lot of relationships go bad. I dated one girl my 11th and 12th year but while I was at college my first year she got pregnant by someone else. I dated one girl for about nine months and then figured out we were not made for each other. I had some other flings that just were not with people I wanted to marry. Well I became frustrated at one point and I left the church-I was a preacher going to Bible college-I'll send you a testimony. I just got done writing that girl I was in love with for two years and got beat to the punch with. The guy chickened out a few weeks before the wedding. She's been out on like two or three dates since then and that was about eight or ten years ago. She is a beautiful woman too. Very sweet, strong in the faith, smart, good job. She is frustrated now I should have stuck it out. We just got separated by college and bad timing. Better think about that! But have faith God is in control. Work hard and be steady- don't quit ever, unless it's for something better or steadier.

  Well I don't have a date yet (It's a joke). But it probably wont be too long. We are locked down here 24-7. It's not like Texas Death Row. We get a three hour yard call each week in separate pens 15'x12', like dog pens. I know just about everybody here. Most don't want to hear the gospel. There are about 20 that probably want to throw away your letters.

The rest hate faith and God and just would write you to ask for money. There are some people here that need encouragement. Some study the Bible to pick it apart and argue about it. Half of the guys here won't respond but you will plant a seed.

    All right-God Bless
        Clay 7-2-00

Brother Mike,   9-2-00

    Well you got put on the back shelf of my writing list. Partly because you said to wait and I wanted to send you some of my newest sermons that the Lord gave to me. So anyway prison can be a very fertile ground to write huh? I mean I can't go anywhere, I'm locked down 24-7's in an 8'x10' cell, the only thing that really brings me joy is studying the Word and prayer. Just think how good your grades would be if there were no student center or gym or bowling, or girls to chase and you were chained to your desk until after class and you meals were slid in under the door. They'd be pretty good huh. You'd had read all your text and suggested reading and be crying for another book already. You better study or God might lock you down. Hee hee. What classes are you taking this semester? What year are you? How big is the college? Do you have chapel everyday, dress code and all that? When I get some more copies of my sermons I'll send you some. I may have someone from the outside send them. Well I'll holler at you later. Keep the faith.

                                        Clay Smith

Mike,   9-14-00

    Well I am glad you are doing ok. Thanks for the letter. No I don't mind answering any of your questions at all. What's up now? Well I am trying to think to write this letter which is a little hard because some guys are arguing pretty loud but I am a pro now at ignoring noise. I have a tree frog in my cell. I fed him a fly earlier now he is sleeping stuck on my window. You know the commercial that advertises a car with four wheel traction or something and they show a tree frog sliding on a window saying he doesn't have the feature the car does? Well my frog does have it.

    My major was preaching and evangelism. I was a junior when I quit. I was involved in a nursing home ministry, teen challenge (a drug program), street witnessing, church visitation, I did two spring impacts to D.C. and Detroit- Helped birth a church there. I'd preach at home some 250 miles away. When I left the ministry and church I did carpenter work and welded and dealt drugs mainly, I also did a lot of other types of work. I didn't do steady work much. I'd make a lot of money quick and draw unemployment for a while. What do I miss? Life! Everything! Family, work, a hope of having my own family, real food. Besides my family, all that is dead. I hardly even dream of it much. I just look forward to Heaven man. Sounds sad huh? I'm not even dismayed- I mainly focus on the Word and pray a lot and I'm really ok. I don't think I have long. I'm probably as happy as a lot of people in the world (outside). I'm 30 years old and I've done about everything except go to the West Coast, Alaska, Hawaii, and Africa and Europe or be officially married. I've been locked up since March 26th, 98, two and a half years. I have a wonderful family, six brothers. Most are married and have kids and have jobs or companies. One brother has about five or six companies. One is a cop and one is a Bandito from way back (that'd be opposite of a cop). My mom and dad are divorced. I don't talk to him much- he owns a construction company. My mom and step dad are retired and travel a lot. I saw them today. I have a good mama.

Well I put my little green friend in a box and had a guard set it next to the door. Actually he was almost yellow because I had him on a yellow bowl for a little while. He could change from a dark green to a yellow green. That was fun. I think they have to eat pretty steady or they die. He only ate a fly today. That was neat to watch. That would be pretty fun to be able to jump about 30 times your length and stick to anything. I could jump the fence and stick to a truck and be gone. I could find one of those low flying twin engines heading to N.Y. and jump on and come see ya Huh. Well I need to go. I got some more sermons to send you and a poem I wrote. God bless you brother.

       Clay Smith

Mike,   10-18-00

I'm doing pretty good. I got a shower last night so I'm happy. We went 6 days without a shower. Our water was off in our cells. Three days we had to smell our own poo poo. The showers are still broke in this barracks. They have been broke several times and we go down to isolation barracks and use their showers but they lied to us and told us they were broke too because they don't care and are lazy and didn't want to take us down there. Well when some people found out they flooded the barracks using the toilets. It was about two inches in my cell. My feet were wrinkled and I stunk. I started making cell boats and floating them past the door of the next cell, a little Mexican dude.

Well the floor is dry again and now I am clean. What can I see from my window? Not much. The window is about four inches wide and four feet tall. But it is in the middle of about a foot and a half of bricks which limits the view. The walls are thick. I can't put my nose on the window cause the frame is only 4 inches wide. I can see a patch of grass for 50 feet then there is a building. Looking over the building is just sky. The 2nd and 3rd floor can see over the building and they see houses and trees over there. When we go on our three hour yard call a week we can see around the buildings.

By the way I have a friend on the outside who has a lot of my stuff on the Internet. His name is Frank. He murdered a lot of people while on drugs in Illinois and did 14 years and got out and is an evangelist now. He has a powerful testimony-Amazing!

What would I do in my first 24 hours free? I'd go to a certain church and grab hold of an alter and pray with deep cries and groans till I passed out and then do it all over again. 1st month? I'd fish with my brothers and spend some time with my nephews and niece and then travel with an evangelist friend of mine. 1st year? Unless God told me different, I'd either work with my dad on his company to get to know him better or better yet let him know me and what God has done. I'd be an evangelist part time and youth pastor or pastor. I'd raise money and build this place out in the country for distressed woman that could be an induction center for women with life controlling problems. It would be based a lot like teen challenge with both a educational plan (Bible training and counseling) along with a vocation program. The women would learn a good work habit. I want to have cows and chickens. I want a large farm. That wouldn't be the vocation program. That would be to teach responsibility and support the place. I want to teach computer skills or whatever the person was interested in-we'd help them pursue it. We would help them find a job and of course a church and solidly set them on their feet. There are programs like this but hardly none for women. Well, I need to get busy on some sermons. Take care brother.
      Clay Smith

Hey Mike,   10-22-00

I don't have time to write a real letter. I'm trying to watch the Olympics. Terrible ain't I? I let the tree frog go and since then I've had about five or six come up to the window on the outside. I'd never had even one come up before I caught the one on the yard and brought it in. Maybe he went and told the rest of them "Hey that guy in 11 cell is a nice guy, go by his window and see him". You reckon? Well there is one on my window this very minute. He is very dark brown. The paint around the window is green and the bricks are dark brown. I guess he sees the bricks and changed to brown. He's a young one maybe he hasn't figured out the art of camouflage real well.

Hey I liked your poetry. I had read the Ping-Pong one before in an earlier letter but not the NIV one. I liked the NIV one. I read them on the toilet. Pray for me bro! These police are really getting on my nerves the last few days. And I'm trying not to hate on them. I just knocked one out and stabbed another and blew up the whole building in my mind and I don't like being in misery. I like Gods peace that surpasses all understanding. Pray for me. Peace- Clay

Mike,   10-30-00

I was so glad to hear about you preaching. That is great man. I also preached the other night here on the row. I preached for about an hour, mainly quoting scriptures very loudly till my voice was gone. We have a man here on the row who is a heretic preacher. He can quote a lot of scriptures but he twists them. He preaches freedom to sin all the while he is a slave to sin. It's the same doctrine Peter and Paul dealt with. He also preached that God is dead! Saying the lamb was slain. He actually leads people astray. He can quote a lot of scripture and can out argue most people. He is very slippery. He's been on Death Row 21 years (longer than anybody here). Picture me shouting the scriptures at the top of my voice, emphasizing the good parts and repeating them over and over. The dude was calling me a liar. I was just quoting. People were cheering and saying take that Satan. This kinda mess goes on around here all the time except it's usually people just cursing not reading the Word unless it's dude blaspheming and preaching heresy. Dude is by far the most vocal in here. He is very loud and screams and hollers every day. He has been quiet lately on the religious stuff. He will come back out on it for sure. Pray for me. Pray the enemy is shut down dysfunctional and defeated and cast out. Pray for Gods work to be done here.

I am facing several intense spiritual battles. Have your people pray for me and these things. A lady wrote me from New Hampshire today who I believe is in the occult. She sent me a picture of herself on her bed in some kinda black thing. It was gross. She is 55 and looks 70 and is a big ol' girl. She says she is into astrology and Halloween is her favorite holiday. She may be a witch or something. I started a fast before I wrote her. I think she is going to get saved and set free. Also the election is very important. Vote for Bush! Please, the abortion issue, you know its murder! A mother does not have the right to kill her baby before it's born. It's murder. Besides Gore is a habitual liar. Did you hear him on the 1st debate claiming to have been in Texas after the fires? Then when busted out about it he claimed "I thought I was there" Yeah right! That night they made a joke about him lying so much on the late night show. He is slimy.

I just had yard call for two hours. I was out there talking to my Mexican buddy. I've been scribing scriptures from a Spanish-English Bible and giving them to him. Remember in your weakness Jesus is strong. Let God lead you. Preach the Word, preach with heart. Love ya bro. Hang tough for Jesus.

   Clay Smith

Mike,   1-31-01

God's hand is on me. I've put in some 12-hour plus days lately, writing, doing research and getting stuff done. I'm pretty organized for a change-got a tight ship. I got rid of a lot of my rough draft sermons and old mail, I sent it home. I'm focused and flowing.

I think they read a lot of the mail that comes in here but not all of it. We have a lot of mail come in and out. Why? Are you trying to witness to the mail room people? Ha Ha-I know you pretty well Huh?

I've been praying for you some but I've kinda been focused on some other folks lately. I prayed pretty hard for you the other day as I read your letter and a few other times. Pray for the prison and the people here around me. Pray for a harvest of souls in China, India, the Islands of the seas etc.

Don't grow tired in your labor of love Mike. Pray for strength, don't become prideful but consider your work as only your reasonable service-it is. Keep encouraging, keep studying. Pray God gives you skill-Microeconomics, Taxation of the Manager, Journalism. Be good at it-it may give you a strategic foothold one day. Be righteous, be Holy.

 Love ya Bro. God Bless You.
   Clay Smith

Mike,   2-20-01

Hey Buddy, Your last letter was a good one. I appreciate the encouragement you have given me over the last few months. You have blessed me. I know you're storing treasure in Heaven. I would love to go to Kenya with you. I read about Africa in Time magazine a week ago. They have a terrible AIDS epidemic. Over 25 million have it in those countries at the bottom of Africa. I have a friend who went to Tanzania a couple of weeks ago. He said lots of people got saved. He said they would stand out in the heat and walk miles to hear the gospel. He said they were drinking the Word in. Said it would make you mad when you come back here and preach in the states.

Well my case was heard by State Supreme Court on mandatory appeal. I will probably get a date the 1st or March for the 1st of May. I got really excited with the thought of going home. I got to thinking about seeing the Lord and talking with Isaiah and Daniel and my brothers and sisters from all ages and parts of the world. I got so excited trying to maintain one morning, it was dead quiet in here but I was jumping up and down with my hands raised. Its almost over, my race is almost complete! Then I realized what I've been thinking for a long time. I got a lot of work to do, so pray bro! I'm not sure why he is using me of all people. I mean I'm a convicted child murderer. It looks like he'd use a TV preacher or something.

    Well I need to go bro. Be sure and pray. Pray for my mom and my step dad too. I am praying for you and your roomies. May God bless you and keep you and make His face shine on you.

    Clay Smith~~Mercy and Grace

P.S. I'll tell you what I'm having put on my tombstone.

The worst of sinners washed in His blood
Absent from the body and in His presence above
With the bride groom sudden
We'll come by to meet the faithful in the air
We'll be in Heaven; those not ready will be left here
Armageddon ends and the King sets foot back here
We resurrected mortals with the Savior reign 1,000 years
The wicked and righteous and the separation is complete

New earth! New Heavens! Eternity is so sweet!

I'm still working on it though.

Mike,   3-20-01

I was starting to wonder when you'd write. I figured you were busy studying. I had a kinda stressful day. I got up at 4:15am and prayed and read my Bible and put my breakfast in a bowl and put my tray back in the door and went back to sleep till 6:45am. That's when my day usually starts. I study the Bible and take notes until about 11:00. Lunch comes about that time. Then I switch gears and start working on something. At 1:20 I had a visit with my brother and his wife and two kids. Visit lasted until 4:30. I watched the news and at my dinner tray and made two egg sandwiches out of my breakfast and turned around and ate a can of spaghetti and meatballs that I warmed up on my light bulb. I wish I had a pillow and a big old window! You think I'll have a view from where I am going-Hmmm-I think so.

I have a friend that's 17 from PA I've been writing. She wrote me and told me she was sexually active and wanted to know what I thought. I wrote her "right back" like she asked and told her it was wrong and that she was removing herself from a place where God could bless her and opening up herself for evil. I don't think she wants to change. I told her she couldn't without Gods help.

My stay of execution has been lifted. The governor should set a date any day. It will be within 60 days of the date he sets it. Well I need to go now. God bless you and your roommates and the people at floor devos. Pray for me OK.

    Clay Smith

Mike,   3-25-01

I just wanted you to know I got my date. It's May 8th. I just wrote you a letter a few days ago so I'm not going to say a whole lot.

Can you imagine looking at Jesus and touching Him for real? Not a dream or a vision but being physically in His presence. What heart felt love! What Joy! 44 more days.

Pray for my family, as I need to be able to hear the Lord clearly. I want to do what he wants me doing every hour. I am hoping he wanted me writing these letters. Pray I am led by the spirit and I have a chance to witness in all of this. Pray for my family. My mom and step dad and my brothers and their wives and children and my step dads children and their families. My dad is probably taking this the hardest. He is lost and it's all gloom and despair to him. I have not talked to him in a long time but my brothers said that's what's up. So pray for him too.

Well I'm going to close. God bless you brother. Keep the shield of faith up.

    Your friend,
      Clay Smith

Mike,   4-9-01

Thanks for the picture. Well I'm glad you're excited for me because I'm excited too. My joy seems to increase everyday. I've been in a real good mood the last few days. I got to expand my phone list and I've been enjoying talking to some new folks. My dad is supposed to come see me this week. Pray for him, he seems to be pretty tore up. Most of my other family is doing pretty good. I've been praying for you missions trip finances and your roommates and floor devos. Do you have dorm prayers too?

Well brother I'm sorry this is a thin one. I think we got time to probably write two more times. I got 29 days. I just wanted to tell you I am doing good. Thanks for the pictures and prayers. I love you bro.

I still got two letters I haven't read from the mail yet. You were the first-aww-ain't dat special. Hee hee hee.

Keep holding up the shield of faith and praying for the saints.
    Clay Smith

Mike,   4-23-01

What's up bro! I got your 2nd letter today. I got you on the list for mama to send my sermons to after I'm gone. I think I told you Janet sounds good. If the girl likes you cool but if not forget her. You know it was because of feelings about a girl I fell out of Bible school. I got depressed, burnt out and gave up on God. Looking back now I'd be patient. If you stay faithful the Lord will reward you. Focus on the Lord

Well I need to go. I got a lot to do and a little time to do it.
    I love you Bro. I'll see you in Heaven.
      Clay Smith

Mike, 4-30-01

    I don't have any pictures right now but we are supposed to get pictures made on my last visits. You can get with my mom after I'm gone and she can help you.

    It's good to hear from you. Janet sounds like a good girl-To hear you talk anyway. Oh my I've been praying for you some.

    Well this is most likely my last letter. I need to get a few things done. I have visits everyday the last five days. I'm feeling great. I get excited when I stop and think about Hebrews 12:22 "But ye are come unto mount Sion, and unto the city of the living God, the heavenly Jerusalem, and to an innumerable company of angels". I love you Mike and I'll see you soon and very soon.

    Clay Smith

Clay's Eulogy

    Well, I hope ya'll are not sad about that old carcass I used for 30 years. I've got news for you. That's not me and I'm glad to leave it behind. I'm in Heaven with Jesus and I guarantee you I'm not sad, so rejoice with me. Weep for yourselves if you want. I know Walt and Robby are jealous, but you guys will finish one day, too.

    I've probably been doing a continuous flip and tumble rejoicing and rolling around in the heavenly grass like a dog that just got dipped. I've probably forgotten all ya'lls requests to ask God to send buck deer by your deer stands or to let you catch 10-pound Bass and all the grandmas I was supposed to say hi to.

    No, you can put half a suit on that body. Barry, you can stick my old finger in its nose, bury it, or whatever you want. I really don't care. I'm going to get a new body one day at the resurrection. I'll meet you in the air if you're still down here—You better be ready.

    In case there are some present who have been taught wrong, I am with Jesus and I'm not in some spiritual coma, soul sleep, or purgatory. 2nd Corinthians 5:6-8 says, "To be absent from the body is to be present with the LORD." Jesus told the thief on the cross, "Today you will be with me in Paradise." Hebrews 12:23 "But you have come to Mount Zion, to the heavenly Jerusalem, the city of the living God. You have come to thousands upon thousand of angels in joyful assembly, to the children of the first born (that's me), whose names are written in heaven (that's me). You have come to God, the judge of all men, to the spirits of righteous men made perfect (that's me now), to Jesus, the mediator of a new covenant…"

I'm in his presence now and it says, "In his presence is fullness of joy and at his right hand are pleasures forever more." I'm with Jesus and that's who I want you to think about. Use the sermons and the book God gave me to write. That's good stuff, but move on please. Forget those things which are behind you and press on toward the mark the heavenly calling in Christ Jesus. If you're right with God by the blood of Jesus, we will see each other again. Rejoice that I've gone home. I did the right thing in death not dragging the victims' families through the courts. You should always do what's right, keep life simple, love God, family, and church. Put your eyes on Jesus, the author and finisher of your faith. My race is over. I kept the faith. I fought the good fight these past few years. Now there is in store for me the crown of life. I didn't continue to sin but turned to God. That's the difference. You're called to live a holy life to be sanctified continually. Don't be deceived. "He who does right is righteous, he who does what is evil is of the devil." Read 1st John Chapter 3. There is a difference in meeting Jesus on the road and following him. You have to follow Jesus. Lay aside the weights of sin and run the race Jesus marked out for you. The race isn't to the swift or strong but for those that endure till the end. Stay in the Word. Read it every day. Keep praying and do the work God has given you to do. Find out what God's will for your life is. The Bible says if you live a pure life you will know God's will. You will be lead by the Spirit. Continue in the faith and do God's will and we will see each other soon. I love you. Clay.

ARKANSAS-execution Clay Smith 5/8/01

As his execution date neared, a killer wrote to his victims' families, promising them he wouldn't pursue any appeals unless they asked.

They didn't.

Instead, these still-grieving mothers and fathers spent Tuesday hoping Clay King Smith wouldn't break his vow. They remained skeptical of Smith's intentions, believing he simply was tormenting them yet again, this time by trying to make them feel responsible for his fate.

"I believe he was wanting us to ask him to appeal it, but I ain't going to do it," Randy Erwin said Monday, the eve of Smith's execution. Erwin's 20-year-old daughter, Misty, was killed three years ago when Smith went on a bloody rampage at the couple's home in rural Jefferson County. Also murdered were Misty's cousin, two nieces and a baby sitter.

Their blood-soaked bodies were found on March 25, 1998, scattered throughout the couple's two-bedroom mobile home.

"He's wanting us to forgive him, saying he won't appeal unless we ask him to. Why would we ask him to do that? I really don't have no mercy on him," Randy Erwin said.

"I hope he don't decide to appeal it anyway," he added. "All he's going to do is tear these families apart more and more. One day I will forgive him -- when he's in the ground."

At 9 p.m. Tuesday, Smith, 30, kept his promise, refusing even at the final hour to pursue appeals still open to him. Had he changed his mind, Smith only had to say so, and the execution would have been halted.

Smith was executed by lethal injection and was pronounced dead at 9:07 p.m.

Asked if he had any final words, Smith said, "Yes, I'd like to say I'm sorry about what I did to the victims' families. I hope your hearts can heal."

Smith's attorney, Tammy Harris, said her client never wavered in his decision not to appeal. "I would say he has made his peace and was resolved to go forward with the execution."

His death will bring peace to some family members. But for others, it will leave questions forever unanswered. Why did this former Bible College student find it necessary to kill not only his girlfriend, but also her cousin and 3 young children?

The mother of one victim corresponded regularly with Smith, to no avail. And the killer's letters to the Erwin family have yielded no clues.

"He wrote a 5-page letter," Randy Erwin recalled. "Hell, I didn't really read it because the one great big old question that everybody asked wasn't answered. Why did he do what he done? He has not, he never will, he will die without telling us. But there's not a reason in this world good enough to explain what he done."

The catalyst that prompted Smith to storm through his home, armed with a .22-caliber semi-automatic rifle, remains unknown.

On March 23, 1998, a deputy was called to the couple's home to help Misty Erwin remove her belongings, according to testimony from Smith's trial. But Smith offered to leave instead, and despite the deputy's urgings that Misty go to a women's shelter, she decided to stay.

Her body was found two days later.

Misty Erwin was a good-natured girl, one of four daughters who had been brought up on a farm before moving to Star City in 1986, her father says.

He's not sure exactly how his daughter met Smith -- possibly at church, he theorizes -- but Randy Erwin said he could tell almost immediately that Misty had gotten herself into a bad relationship. "I was worried to death," he said, recalling the month during which Smith refused to let anyone see or talk to Misty. "And now my daughter's dead and gone. My niece and her babies, they're all gone."

He doesn't know how or why Misty's cousin, Shelly, happened to be visiting at the time of the murders.

"They were pretty close," he said. "Shelly was just out there spending the night, and this guy just went crazy, I guess. He went all through the house shooting. He is the devil. There's no such thing as going down to meet the devil -- he is the devil."

When Smith was captured by law enforcement officers on March 26, 1998, he offered no explanation for the murders other than he was on drugs at the time.

"I sent three of them to heaven. I don't know where the hell the other two went!" he shouted during a tense, armed standoff with police. "I wish I could take a couple of days back. I was on drugs. I was high."

Smith's spiritual adviser, the Rev. Robby Mitchell of Texarkana, said Smith blamed his drug addiction and demon worship for what he did. Smith never said, however, exactly what had made him angry enough to kill five people, Mitchell added.

In his letters to the Erwin's, Smith talked of finding God in prison -- a claim Randy Erwin scoffs.

"He's supposed to have gotten saved. He may fool some people here on Earth, but I don't believe he can double-cross the good Lord. He can be the best Christian man from now on, but he still can't bring back what he took from us."

Randy Erwin and other family members watched the execution on closed-circuit television at the Cummins Unit, where Arkansas' Death penalty is carried out.

Despite Smith's efforts to reach out to the family, Randy Erwin still wanted him to die, because as long as Smith was alive, the anger and hatred would linger.

"I think I can pretty well forgive him once he's dead. We won't have to worry about him no more."
(Arkansas Democrat-Gazette, Newspaper 2001)

What it's like being on the drug Meth, in Clay Smith's words:

When you are on Meth, you're like a dumb deer mesmerized by the headlights of an on-coming car. You are standing in the path of destruction and will be run over. The word "witchcraft" comes from the Greek work pharmakia (pharmacy) i.e. drug use, sorcery, black magic, worship of demons and use of drugs to produce spiritual experiences. Drugs open one up to spiritual things. They put you in the spirit world. You keep Demon Company. Your will becomes weak and you become seduced by demonic spirits. They will dupe you into believing conspiracy theories about the government or maybe your loved ones. The next step is paranoia and suspicion. These demons are powerful and not just spring chickens. They are angry and plant ideas of murder and revenge in your mind. The moral value system begins to break down. Things that were once wrong are OK when high on Meth. You steal in broad daylight thinking with the prevailing thoughts that it belongs to you. You become loose in your sexual activities.

You are being schooled by demons that have been around for thousands of years. They are the masters of deceit. They are very wicked. You learn to cheat and lie to yourself as they toy with you. You are the enlightened one; smarter and clever, but pride is planted in your heart. Thinking you are up on all the schemes, the wicked spirits are designing the schematics of your life. Your network of associates is likewise a tool of Satan and his hierarchy of evil. All have been influenced by this dark regime of evil. Meth is the common denominator linking this network. Some feel important while delusions of inferiority and loss of respect warp other personalities. But all are slaves and are playing a losing game. Always, whatever the role that is played, it all comes crashing down. The evidence is moral depravity, financial disaster and decay, and devastation to families. This doesn't seem to matter to one who is 'hooked' on crystal Meth.

As the false anointing increases, the hooks sink in more deeply. Sometimes the devil grants supernatural gifts to his students. These abilities and physic powers cause one to be powerful, important and wise. In reality you're only weaker and foolish listening more intently to the familiar spirits. You have become a puppet of the devil.

Meth will destroy your life. Your morals, relationships and work ethics rapidly crumple to nothing. You will be abused spiritually, physically, and socially. The Devil comes to steal kill and destroy. You can be faithful to him but he will never be faithful to you. Satan's promises are a lie. He will forsake you. He will kill you given the chance. He hates everybody without exception.

The only hope is God's amazing grace and mercy. There is an escape. The answers are the gospel of Jesus Christ. The blood shed on the cross can wash you clean. The Word of God can restore your mind and bring you to your senses. Jesus holds the key to set you free. Talk to Him.

This is a written excerpt that Clay wrote a short time before he died.

Today I hear a lot of people say that they believe in God because there is definitely a higher power in control. To some people evolution has become a religion. The clever people decided to invent stories of man evolving from a single cell. That's like saying a tornado went through a junkyard and built a perfectly operational 747-jet. I suppose believing a lie is the answer to the unknown to a lot of people. Thinking you know something is way easier then saying I don't know and having to search for the truth.

I believe I know the truth. I believe that the God of the Bible is God. I believe that He spoke what we see into creation just as He said in the Bible. I've been reading the Bible for 12 years now. It never ceases to, amaze me. There have been times when I questioned its authority and even thought I found discrepancies in it, but with further studying and with the help of God my questions got answered. I also found out that I was wrong and there are no discrepancies in it. I can honestly say that I personally know our Creator. Let me tell you how he made Himself known to me.

I was 15 years old. I had poor morals. I used drugs and I was a bit on the wild side. One day while I was playing my guitar, something started speaking to my heart and mind. It was the Devil. Somehow I just knew it was. I'd hardly ever gone to church my whole life. Maybe five times total. I had never been told by anyone about God or Satan personally, but I knew who it was. He told me that if I served him he would give me my desires. My middle name is King and I just figured I'd be my own king and serve only myself.

A little while later I was walking out of the house and God spoke in my mind to me. I looked up and saw the moon. As I was looking up God asked me, "can you make a moon in the sky like you see or a sun?" I knew I couldn't. He said, "How will you be God then?" I don't remember why but I went back in the house and got a Bible. I took it outside and went down a little trail in the woods behind the house. I opened it to the book of John and sat on a log and read. At 15 years old and being a 10th grader, I had an elementary school reading level. I had high scores in math and science, but I had a learning disability with reading. I was dyslexic. When I was asked to read in class, it would take two minutes for me just to read a few sentences. I never comprehended what I was reading. I learned mainly by hearing or seeing. That day I read quickly and clearly. I read the first 14 chapters of the book of John that day. If you had been my mom or one of my school teachers, you would have said it was a miracle.

It wasn't long before I read the Bible completely through. I began going to church and before long I got saved.

During my junior and senior years of high school, I spent my Christmas vacations on mission trips to South America with other young people. Before long I went to Bible College and became a youth pastor. I helped with work in the inner cities and help plant churches there. I had many spiritual battles and had countless prayers answered. Over a period of many years I walked with God.

There came a point when I walked away from the Lord. I always felt close to the Lord, as if He had shown me special attention. When I prayed and asked God for things, I saw my prayers answered most of the time. I remember praying for years for God to give me a helpmate, a wife. I had some close relationships for a year or two but things never seemed to work out. We would be separated by circumstances or things would come between us that we sometimes couldn't work out. . I became discouraged and angry with God. This had a lot to do with me then leaving the church I was attending and my stopping of reading the Bible. Before long I changed my morals back to the old ways.

There's a spiritual war going on, when you are on the front lines ministering for God you better not forget where your strength comes from or take your focus off of God. The Devil hates everybody and is a great deceiver. He truly hates everybody; some just don't know it because he is such a great deceiver.

I hate to give Satan's team a victory report, but for about five years I served the Devil and myself. I asked Satan for the things I wanted and he gave them to me. I did my best to silence the voice of God in my mind and my heart by using drugs, alcohol and music. Eventually I didn't hear the voice of God anymore. I became engrossed with evil. I learned the Devils ways used the gifts of talent, which God had given me, for evil.

The Devil deceived me with his lies until a little over a year ago. I was in a diagnostic prison hospital facing five counts of capital murder. I'd been shot in the arm trying to get the authorities to kill me rather then take me in. Because of Gods hand on my life, I was spared from death several times. It had been many years since I heard the Lord speak to me. I gave my life back to God. My life had been wrecked my sin and the devil. My mind was gone, I was nuts and my body was wrecked. My arm had nearly been shot off by a high-powered rifle. My leg had a twelve-inch cut where doctors took a vein out to put in my arm. I lost about sixty pounds over a short period of time. I lost my freedom and my family. But I was better off then I had been in a long time. The suffering inside and out was beyond measure. But the Lord was speaking to me again. I got a Bible and began reading it night and day. The Lord renewed me mind and cleaned me up spiritually.

Right now I am sitting on Death Row and about to be executed soon. This may sound sad to you, but to me it is exciting. Yes, I said exciting. Exciting because I know that when I die I'll be with Jesus, my Lord, in paradise. Scriptures says for the saved, and I am saved, "We are confident, I say, and willing rather to be absent from the body, and to be present with the Lord." It says, "But as it is written, eye hath not seen, nor ear heard, neither have entered into the heart of man, the things which God hath prepared for them that love him."

I could honestly fill the pages off the top of my head with promises that God gives to His children concerning the afterlife. I believe Gods Word. He has never lied to me. This life is nothing but a test of your faith. God deals with each of us in his own way. I feel very special. Yes, I have fallen short many times. I betrayed God. I was a very sinful child. A wild teenager. I even turned my back on the ministry of showing others how to be saved. I know I haven't deserved His love, grace and mercy but I am very thankful for it. I fell I deserved to die in my sins and should spending and eternity in Hell right now. God spared me and I repented. It is His grace that did this. I want to give Him all the praise and glory for all He has done.

I can hardly wait for this life to be over. I have absolutely no fear at all of death but I long for it. The trial of this life will be over and gone. I'll inherit an eternity in heaven with the one who loves me the most, God my Savior. Sin will never separate me from God again. My sinful nature will be gone. I'll receive a new body. One that is immortal, imperishable, powerful and glorified.

God the creator of the universe reduced me to nothing. He humbled me and brought me to my senses. I thank God for grace and for having mercy on me. I'm forever His child and He watches over me.

Clay became a citizen of Heaven the day he got saved and became a resident the day he was put to death. I was able to call his mother a short while after the execution. She was excited to tell me how seven people, at Clays funeral, raised their hands during a time of invitation saying how they would like to be saved. I also got word that his father is curious about salvation now too.

His letters and poems were an inspiration to many students at Maranatha Baptist Bible College. I personally looked forward to every morning when the mail was put in our boxes and I would scan through it all to see his name on one of the envelopes. I knew there was something inside that envelope waiting to encourage me. I let many others at the college read his letters. They began to learn more about him after each letter and form a picture in their mind of Clay. A man just like any of us in this world. A sinner who was Hell bound until he realized his need for salvation. Clay was like you and me. He had dreams and desires. Clay had likes and dislikes. Yet even after being locked up in a prison he still found time to reach out and care for others. His testimony is still being used by God to bring others to know Christ as their Savior.

Jeff Dillingham

This former video store manager was drawn away and enticed with the lust of money. This 19-year-old high school graduate was just another regular teenager. He was fronted with the opportunity to make one million dollars by killing two people and took the offer.

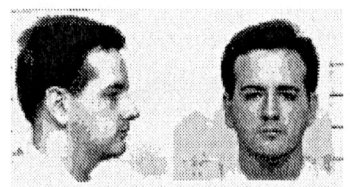

Source: www.tdcj.state.tx.us/index.htm 9/5/01

Dear Mike,   7-14-00

      Hello! I received your most welcomed letter tonight. I pray that I find you in the very best of health and spirits. I am doing great. Your letter was a great surprise and blessing. I truly gave my life to Christ on Sept. 26, 1999 and know exactly what you mean because that very night he took away all my loneliness and depression. I wasn't even totally free of that in the world and I actually had a pretty good life. You did a really good job on this letter. I have gotten a few since I have been locked up and they are always really judgmental and to be honest actually hateful. Your letter seemed very sincere and kind and I thank you for that. It gave me great encouragement to because more and more I am trying to be bold for Christ so I got a good charge out of your letter.

      You point out sin (Isaiah 53:6) but you didn't try to make me feel like I was the only sinner in the world or the worst. How would I answer God? I would plead the blood of Christ. That I have been given eternal life, not by anything I have done but by the grace of God. John 5:24, 1stPeter 2:24, Colossians 2:14, Romans 9:16. I really thank you for this letter, for your boldness. To me it is the perfect example of 2ndTimothy 4:2. I pray you will continue to write and that we can become close friends.

      It is funny; you are an answer to prayer. I have been asking God for someone I could fellowship with. I have good people in my life but I mean someone I can really talk about and share Christ with. I knew religion all my life, I was raised a Catholic and have been a "religious" person to varying degrees. I got really religious when I got locked up. A man gave me a Bible and encouraged me and read with me. I later got my Bible sent in and spent a lot of time studying the Word. Did not realize my error though, I had only ever known "religion". I was moved to do an extended fast and I did. I read through the Bible in 39 days and on Sept. 26, 1999 I gave all of my life to Christ. I told Him that everything I had, everything I was or wanted to be I threw away. Everything I am or ever will be I give to you (God). For the first time in my life I was free of loneliness and depression, for the first time I could feel God and knew who He was. (Actually had a relationship with Him now). My wife and I had split and it was a really hard thing for me, I loved her so much. That was the catalyst. My eyes filled with tears and that is when I told Him that I gave myself to Him. I took off my wedding ring and have never worn it since. Even sent it home. We split about the time you found Christ; the last time I saw her was March 31, 1995. It has been amazing since then too. He has taught me so much and done so much for me. I even keep a blessing journal now just to try to keep up. Believe me, you made it on to today's entry!

  I am 27, my birthday is March 6th. I am 6'4" and have dark hair (with lots of gray). Finished high school and half a semester of college (took a "W") and pulled out for work. Been married once but no children. I used to paint but they took that away from us in March 99. If you have any questions ask. I would love to know more about you and I really do hope you will write and we can be friends. Don't feel you have to though, I want you to be my friend because I am a fellow brother in Christ, not out of pity cause of my being on Death Row.

  I guess I will close this up for now. When do you go back to school? Where is Watertown? Please take good care of yourself. Thank you again for the letter, it was great getting to meet you. I am enclosing a copy of a photo of my mother and I. Please keep it. Know I have added you to my prayer list and will be keeping you in all my prayers. God Bless You! Have a great day!

  En Philia,
   Jeff

Dear Mike,   8-4-00

  Was glad to hear back from you. I pray all is well on your end. God is taking great care of me. I am hoping to catch you before you go off to school. Thank you for the verse, I enjoyed them. My favorite for this situation is Psalm 37:7 "Rest in the LORD, and wait patiently for him".

    En Philia,
        Jeff

Dear Mike,   9-21-00

    Hello! How are you today? God has blessed me with an abundance of opportunities to share Christ lately. Praise God! I love to serve Him. Get this, a lady in California who started to write me wanted to send me money. She didn't have much but wanted to do something. Praise God if she didn't get $100 raise right before she sent me some. $50 for me and $50 for her. God gave her 2 ½ times what she planned to send me. God is amazing. Take care and have a great day. Know you are in my prayers. God Bless You.

    En Philia,
        Jeff

Dear Mike,   10-26-00

    Hello, How are you? I don't expect a pardon until close, if I get one. To me the closer the better. The closer I get the greater witness for Christ. I am glad you liked the photos of the art I did. I miss it at times but now I just have more time to spend with God. The wheat is ripe and white for the harvest my friend. Thank you for the prayers. I will keep you informed as things develop. Well, I guess I will go for now. You take care and study hard. Know I keep you in all my prayers! God Bless You!

    En Philia,
        Jeff

Last Meal:

    One cheeseburger with American, Cheddar and Mozzarella cheese, without mayonnaise, mustard or onions; large French fries; bowl of macaroni and cheese; lasagna with two slices of garlic bread; 4 oz. of nacho cheese; three large cinnamon rolls; five scrambled eggs; eight pints of chocolate milk.

Last Statement:

I would just like to apologize to the victim's family for what I did. I take full responsibility for that poor woman's death, for the pain and suffering inflicted on Mr. Koslow. Father, I want to thank you for all of the beautiful people you put in my life. I could not have asked for two greater parents than you gave me. I could just ask for two greater people in their life now. It is a blessing that there are people that they love so much but even more so, people that I love so much.

I thank you for all the things you have done in my life, for the ways that you have opened my eyes, softened my heart. The ways that you have taught me. For teaching me how to love, for all of the bad things you have taken out of my life. For all the good things you have added to it.

I thank you for all of the beautiful promises that you make us in your Word, and I graciously received every one of them. Thank you Heavenly Father for getting me off of Death Row and for bringing me home out of prison. I love you Heavenly Father, I love you Jesus. Thank you both for loving me.

Amen.

Source: www.tdcj.state.tx.us 9/5/01

Greg Wright #999253

Hello Mike: January 31, 2001

I have a younger brother named Mike so your name will be easily remembered.

I have received your letter dated January 22nd. I have been rather busy with my legal situation, studying statues and case law. I did get a little behind on my letter writing. I apologize but these circumstances required my full attention.

I do appreciate your concern for saving souls from eternal damnation. Please know that I accepted Jesus as my personal savior at the age of 13. I even got baptized!

As an adolescent I attended church on a regular basis. I went to revival meetings and church camps and even summer Bible school.

I quit going to church at the age of 17. I was confused with no guidance. I had a bright future in sports but extraneous circumstances prevented even that from becoming a reality. Through it all I never lost my belief. I just wasn't living with respect to what Jesus and the Bible said we should do regarding worship and moral standards.

I am 35 years young and am currently fighting for my life. The real killer used myself as an escape goat. The court appointed an unqualified attorney to represent my case. I don't think I got a fair trial, but it certainly looks like they mean to kill me regardless. I never did make a statement or testify. I had no real defense at the trial. All of this equals an execution in the state of Texas. It doesn't take much.

I have been building a huge knowledge of the Word of God since I have been here for the last 3 years.

I fall under the new procedural law and the appeal process has speeded up considerably. There are guys that have been her 8-12 years and they are not yet as far as I am in the process. Under these new provisions a convicted case will run through the entire process in 5-6 years. There will be no more cases lasting 10 years or more on Death Row.

Well you probably didn't want to hear all of that but I had to let you know that I am having a lot of difficulty and my poverty seems to be a big part of the equation. Yes I am a sinner, but with Jesus I have cleaned up my act considerably.

        Respectfully, Greg

Hello Mike, February 26, 2001

I am responding to the letter you dated 2/19/01. I am running behind a bit this time due to the lack of funds.

Well, I turned 35 on 11/01/00. I am originally from Tennessee but I went to school in Kentucky. I moved to Tennessee around the age of 21.

My legal situation is this. Around march 23rd I was assaulted by a S.W.A.T. team who was led to believe that I was armed and dangerous. This was back in 1997 in a neighboring county of Dallas, Texas. I exercised my right to keep silent for numerous reasons. None of which related to the case.

The actual killer himself turned himself in and used me as the scapegoat. I lived at the scene of the crime and had circumstantial evidence leading me to the murder.

My trial was almost a year later and I was found guilty on circumstantial evidence and the real killer's statement putting all the blame on me. The only catch was he didn't testify. No cross-examination of the reported statement was given. Still the judge allowed the statement. Add to that an unqualified attorney to my trial. Ignorance of the law is not a legal defense in the state of Texas.

On appeal, I raise up the issue as an error of the trial court. But they said since I didn't object before or during the trial to the appointment of the attorney, then I did not reserve the issue for review by the appeal court.

I have been on Death Row for 3 years. To this date I have not testified at trial or given a legal statement of the events, as I know them. I certainly believe that this state means to kill me within the next 2 years.

All of my family, except my father, don't correspond with me. I have never had a family visit.

I will be praying for your trip to Kenya. You pray for me too and my needs here. God will bless us both.

Thanks for writing Mike. I will promise to pray for you and blessings on this trip. Take care and stay healthy.

Respectfully,
Greg

Susan Atkins

Atkins was once a member of the Manson Family in California. She was determined to be the evangelist for the group and recruiter for the cult. Manson's cult was charged with an overall nine murders and was suspected of approximately a dozen more killings. Atkins took part in the killings. Susan Atkins said that her lover Charlie was Jesus Christ and he was going to lead her to a hole in the earth in Death Valley where there was a civilization down there.

After some time in prison, Atkins came to know Jesus Christ as her Lord and Savior. She became a born-again Christian and follows the Bible.

From Susan Atkins, former Manson Family member, to Kate Woodby [written on a thank-you card]

Dear Kate,   5/4/02

Bless your precious heart. Thank you for your witness of Jesus. On Sept. 27, 1974, perhaps before you were born, I accepted Jesus Christ as my personal savior and Lord. I've been walking with Him ever since, Glory to God.

Your witness and letter truly blessed my heart. May the Lord continue to cause you to grow & serve Him, may you always love Him unto obedience.

Perhaps He's called you to be an evangelist. Whatever your calling and purpose, may the fire of the Holy Spirit in you always be within you & upon you.

Sincerely your sister in Jesus,
Susan

Dear Kate,   June-July 2002

Grace and Peace to you in Jesus Name. Summer is upon us. Outside my new room there is a huge and exquisitely beautiful tree. Every morning the sparrows, finches and English blackbirds gather to chatter about the day's events to come. Sometimes they fuss over territory (room on a branch) and feathers fly. I expect to soon see baby birds following their parents as they hunt for food. The Lord cares for and provides for the sparrows. How much more valuable are you! Surely as you get up each day, He's already made provision for you.

Breaking Barriers with Jesus Christ is moving forward. Praise God! At present we have three sessions going. One of which is for the Spanish speaking women. At one of our sessions three women accepted Jesus for the first time. At the next session the following day another young woman wanted to accept Jesus. The following week as I met for each group's meetings, there was a distinct difference in the women's attitudes. Praise the Lord. As I work with these women in Breaking Barriers with Jesus Christ, it's my hope and prayer that they will come to understand that salvation is the beginning, learning how to live and have a personal and vibrant relationship with Jesus is a daily process that can be exciting and challenging.

As yet Administration of C.I.W. still has not made a decision about my cards and prints. I know they've written a few people who wanted to purchase my cards and prints and told them I wasn't authorized to sell them. The truth is that I was given permission to sell them and later someone in Administration decided that perhaps they should be pulled from me and held until someone in Sacramento (?) could decide if the person who authorized me to sell them did the right thing. Unfortunately this is a reoccurring pattern in the California Department of Corrections. Though it would be illegal for the CDC to officially state that I can not enter authorized programs, there are many programs which I have been unofficially barred from participating in-either my application gets lost over and over, or my name keeps getting dropped from the waiting lists, or the qualifications for the program are changed after they find out I've applied to participate, or as in this case, if I participate they threaten to close down the entire program. As I've already told you, the program and procedure for selling cards and prints has been in place for over two years prior to my involvement and no one in the Administration questioned it until I participated. The true shame, of course, is that these programs are Community Betterment programs-programs which serve a purpose to the community outside prison, either by contributing to programs outside the prison walls, or by helping to treat women in here for repeat offenses so that they can break the cycle of behaviors that keeps bringing them back, or by encouraging young people to avoid the traps which lead to prison. It's now been over three months and no one in authority has said anything to me. As soon as I am advised of their decision I'll share it with you.

Last month Diane Sawyer came to C.I.W. and interviewed the women in the "Long Termers' Organization." I agreed to speak with her on a one to one. this program might be aired on July 11th, 2002 on ABC Prime Time. It was a very difficult interview for me, as Ms. Sawyer wanted to focus on the past and I wanted to focus on the present, the power of redemption through Jesus Christ and the present violations of the law by the Board of Prison Terms and Parole against all California term-to-life prisoners.

Please keep me in your prayers as I move forward with Jesus and move forward in the Court of Law on my writ. I need and covet your prayers.

Our Toastmasters club is doing wonderfully. It's always a challenge to stand up in front of others and give a speech. This week I give my fourth speech, and I have yet to write out what I am going to say. It will probably be about artwork and the process of creative inspiration.

Until next time, may the Lord guide your heart and draw you close to His heart.

I remain your faithful sister in Jesus,
Susan

P.S.-Have you ever heard of the saying 'bloom where you're planted'? Jesus causes us to grow right where he found us. It's His plan to transform us into His image and likeness so God will get glory. He can do that no matter who we are.

Dear Kate,   August 2002

Greetings in the precious Name of Jesus, our Savior, Lord, and soon coming King of Kings.

On July 30, 2002, a very dear friend of mine, Marge Tanner, went home to be with Jesus. Marge has been my friend for 22 years. Her death was sudden and unexpected. Marge was serving a term of 7 years to life with the possibility of parole. She was only 63. She had been given a parole date 12 years ago, but our former Governor took it away from her.

Marge accepted Jesus as her Savior in a county jail before she came to CIW. For as long as I knew Marge she lived to serve her Savior and Lord, Jesus, by serving all who crossed her path. The love of God flowed through her like a river. There was never a time when I didn't see Marge with a smile. She always carried kleenex and candy in her pockets. Why? Because in prison someone is always crying and needs something sweet; Marge was always prepared.

Even though Marge was in prison, her loving compassion for people and her devotion to Jesus touched thousands upon thousands of lives. When the word came to prison that Marge had died, there was a very long sound of silence as tears streamed down the cheeks of prisoners and staff alike. Those who knew Marge know she's with Jesus in Heaven-free!

When Marge left this earth, she left all who knew her and loved her, as well as those who only met her in passing, a legacy and an example of the love of Jesus Christ in action.

Marge was also one of my art teachers and mentors. Her paintings and drawings were part of the reason why I wanted to learn to draw and paint. Her ability to capture the soul of an animal was like anyone else. Every now and then God allows us a glimpse of His grace and compassion in the lives of special people who live it every day. Marge obeyed the commandment Jesus gave us all, "Love your neighbor as yourself." She wasn't a preacher or an evangelist, a healer or a miracle worker, but everywhere Marge walked and worked in prison, her actions proclaimed the gospel Jesus preached, souls were saved, hearts were healed, and miracles of changed lives were her legacy.

I wanted to share with you this month the gift God gave me for 22 years in my friend Marge and to celebrate her life and going home.

The prison will never be the same without Marge. By that I mean, there are now more hugs being given, more kleenex and candy are being carried in pockets in case tears need to be wiped away or someone just needs a little something sweet on a sour day. More smiles and genuine questions of "how are you today," are being asked with more listening ears and compassionate hearts. Marge was never too busy to stop and care about someone else in need.

If you have never met someone like Marge, perhaps you may want to review 1st Corinthians 13:1-13, and ask Jesus to help you become someone like my dear friend and mentor Marge. She was a wonderful Word-waterer. She knew that most people knew about Jesus, and that He came to save the lost. Most prisoners are lost or have backslid. Her mission was to water the Word of God already in her neighbors' hearts with the love of God. Only God knows today how truly effective her life was here at CIW. I see the evidence of it as I watch my neighbors and some of the staff here be more loving, kind and compassionate to each other.

Jesus meant what He said, "A new commandment I give unto you, That ye love one another as I have loved you, that ye also love one another. By this shall all men know that ye are my disciples, if ye have love one to another." John 13:34-35.

My friend lived and died as a true disciple of Jesus Christ. It is my prayer that I will carry on as she did, and my hope that you will too. For the Glory of God and the furtherance of His Kingdom.

PS: Diane Sawyer's ABC Prime Time interviews with the Long Termers' Organization was not shown in July. I have since been told that it will probably be aired sometime after the September 11th specials.

PPS: Please join me this month in a prayer for the families and friends of those touched by the crimes that sent me to prison 33 years ago. Their pain and loss, even to this day, can not be overemphasized, and I would be grateful if you would join me in praying that they be given God's peace in their lives, and that He bless them and those they love.

Sincerely, I remain your faith filled sister in Jesus.
    Susan

Julius Murphy #999279

Date of Birth 10/25/1978

Summary of the Incident:
   On 9/19/97, the subject shot a 26 year old male one time in the head with a .25-caliber semi-automatic weapon during a robbery.

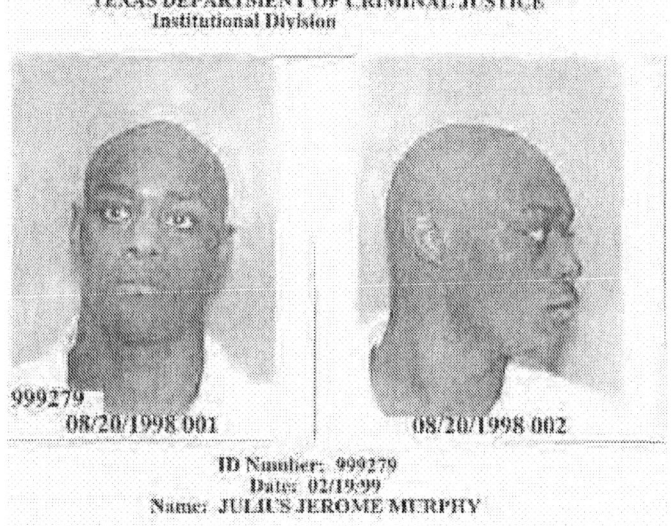

Source: www.tdcj.state.tx.us/index.htm 9/5/01

Dear Mike,   October 12, 2000
   First of all I would just like to thank you for writing to me this letter. I am so very glad that you would write to me concerning the Word of God. I would like to take this time out to tell you I spend a lot of my time reading the Word every day. I grew up in church and have known God for a while personally.
   I found peace with God in so many ways my brother. I am still trying to keep myself in the Word daily because I see so many individuals falling away from God each and every day. I pray for them and I tell them about how good the Lord is and I think a lot of them know it. It's just that when problems come their way they give up on God. I have learned in my life that the more you stay with God, the more that He works in your life.
   I am 21 years old and have read through the Bible over 3 times. I just keep learning about the Bible because you can never learn enough about God and his goodness. I am so glad that I got saved and super happy to know that I am going to go to Heaven once I leave this world. I

know this and believe this with all my heart Mike. I believe everything that the Holy Bible says about anything and everything. I read it each day and learn from it each day. I am never going to give up on God because I know He is never going to give up on me. I am glad to be a child of God.

I am going to close this letter for now and stay cool my brother and may God bless you and your friends.

Sincerely,
Julius Murphy

Dear Mike,   October 29, 2000

Hi there brother! How has everything been coming along for you? I am thankful for all the encouragement you have been sending me. Things can get a little bit hectic down here but I learned that being patient in the Lord is the way to be.

We are on lockdown, for what I don't know. Here is something that I would like you to pray for. This means a lot to me Mike because this is a very close friend of mines baby sister. She is very ill and the doctors don't know what is wrong with her. They think she may have some form of cancer but they are not sure what kind. She was in the hospital for a while because she was bleeding for a while on every end of her body. Now they have her on steroids and that is very stressing for me because she is only 15 years old. I would appreciate you prayers concerning her. Pray for my mom too. She is trying to get this job that she really would like to get. Also that she would stop smoking cigarettes.

Well being it is that you are a child of God as I am I know that we can make our walk with God better through our correspondence. Keep in touch and stay up in God my brother. Take care!

Until then Brother!
Julius

Wednesday   December 6, 2000

Mike,

What's up man! What's been going on with you man? Is all well with you down there these days lately man? Well I am so sorry that it has token me so long to get back to you man. I have just been pressed for time down this way man or, should I say tired. I have been wanting to write to you this letter but, every time that I have the time there comes something else in my way Mike for real. So whenever I am through with whatever I was doing then I be tired and, ready to go to sleep, you know what I mean? So is school and everything going alright down there man? You are in my prayers brother and please know this Mike.

Anyways man how did your Thanksgiving go brother? I hope that everything went well with you and yours my friend. Next Christmas is right around the corner like next door. Man I hope that you have a nice Christian Christmas with your friends and family Mike. I know that this is the time of the year for all of that stuff, don't you think man? I think that what you are doing is really cool because getting to reach people is a very hard job man. And seeing as though you have done a lot with reaching people I would think that this is your calling from God. Well we all have a calling from God for the working of his will in our lives you know brother.

Lately I have been falling into temptation like I don't know what Mike. And I am not trying to keep falling until Satan claims my soul. Although that will never happen because, I know where my heart is at and its going to be with him and that's for real!

Well, I am going to go for now, I will keep in touch with you man. I will also continue to pray for you as well brother. So you keep it cool. May God bless you and yours.

Until Then!

Brother in Christ Jesus,
Julius

Sunday   January 14, 2001

Dear Mike,

Hi there Mike! How's everything been coming along for you these days through the month of Christmas as well as the New Years? I am hoping that everything has been alright for you. I am doing alright, we just came up off of another lockdown down this way. There was so much stuff going that I didn't know anything of. But once again through the Grace of God we were able to make it through the shake downs. I will continue to send out my prayers to you and yours my man.

I will send you some prayer requests because there is a lot of things that I need some prayer for.

So did you get what you were hoping for this Christmas? Well, I sure do hope you did. I got some things from some organizations as well as this church which is so very great. Because I had some homemade cookies and other things such as fruit.

Today is my chilling day from everything. I don't do nothing on Sundays but read my Bible and lay back in this cell all the time on this day.

Prayer Requests:

    1. That my mother is alright because I haven't heard from her in a long time. 2. That my babies mother will find me and let me be able to get to know my daughter. 3. That the Lord will continue to help me in this life of struggling. 4. Pray for all the lost souls in this world. 5. Pray for things to go well with my case this time because it didn't go well the first time around. 6. That all the hate will cease in this world because it is very hurting to me to hear time and time again about something terrifying happening. I thank you for your time in praying for me on all these things here. I will lace you up on some more in time my brother. Take care.

    I will keep in touch as much as seemingly I can. So you stay cool my brother in the Lord and I will keep you in my prayers.

Until Then!

        Brother in Christ Jesus,
            Julius

Dear Mike,   February 15, 2001

    Hi There Bro! How's everything been coming along for you down there these days brother? I am hoping that everything is fine with you as well as for you my man. Well, me I am doing alright I am just flowing with the wind brother. I am so very late, I would like to say "sorry" that it has tooken me so very long to write back my man. But the truth is that I have been tired, lazy, and other things my man. So I ask that you would forgive me for my late letter in response to yours.

    I will be praying that the Lord bless things to go as you have asked them of Him the Lord. Because I know that it can happen because, the Lord is Almighty in everyway. I am grateful that you are doing things in the Lord my man. Because as the Bible says the harvest is plenteous but, there aren't that many laborers for the harvest brother.

    I have been in the word more because I am trying to overcome to the extent all this temptation. I am hoping and I am praying that God would free me physically as well as mentally from the sin I commit. So yes I have some more "Prayer Requests" for you from me my man. And not only for me but, for the people around me that I know and don't know.

I thank you for your prayer's as well as your love in Christ Jesus. I will continue to be praying for you and yours each and everyday. Oh yeah I liked what Mr. Tanis preached on because we all need to be bold in preaching the Word of God. Because we sometimes don't know what to say sometimes. Let alone know how to go about what we want to say. I am continuing to grow in the word but, I have introduced Christ Jesus to some brethren. Some are already saved and some are now saved.

I am thankful I was able by the power of God to do that. Well I don't know about whether he is saved or not. But since I don't know his name I will not call him "The Railroad Killer". Because that isn't right to call him that. I mean I done unto others as I would have them do unto me. Because that is the Christian way don't you think Mike.

Anyways once again the sermon is correct in every sense of the word I love it my man. But yeah! They got those dudes that got away a while back that I hear as well. I have seen it in the papers sometime ago

Oh well I hope that they are saved as well. Anyways my man I am going to close this letter but, I will enclose those prayer requests. And once again I thank you for your prayer's my man. So you take cane down there and keep God close too your heart brother. I will do the same thing and I hope things turn out fine with your trip to Kenya pretty soon.

Prayer Requests:
#1. Pray that God bless me to see my daughter again.
#2. Pray that God bless my brother and sister get married and stop living in fornication out there
#3. Pray that God would help me to become stronger in the power of the spirit to be overcome of temptation.
#4. Pray that God would bless the things that wasn't quite right done too me in my case be changed this time around.
#5. Pray that would bless his word to reach the hearts of our brothers and sisters in this world my man.

These are my prayer requests you can pray for them in any order because, they will all be heard I know and believe God hears all. Take Care!
Brother In Christ Jesus,   Julius

Sunday   March   11, 2001

Dear Mike,

    What's up my brother! How's everything been coming for you down there these days lately? I am hoping that everything is going my man. I received your letter and was very please the power of the spirit is still there. Well, me I have been doing blessed at the most God is by my side too help me overcome the things that I feel so sometimes burdened by. But other than that my man I am still in the word of God.

    Mike there is something that I would like to bring to your attention. Because I want you to know and understand that this isn't right. When you write too me concerning Angel you call him the "Railroad Killer" brother that isn't right in the eyes of God that you call him that. I am not being funny or anything my brother but that is not the "love of Christ." To be labeling him as what the world and man has named him. Because didn't make no railroad killer God made man. So I would really be grateful if you would be nice enough brother buy calling our brother by his name. I would not be your brother in Christ if I didn't bring this too you my man. Brother remember James chapter 3 because it is good that we remain in the truth and keep our mouths from unrighteous things.

    Anyways my man so, you are talking too this girl now. Well, I will pray for you brother but, please I ask that you'll keep yourself from fornication in everyway. And that you put the Lord over this your new found friendship with your new friend. I am so very pleased as well that Mr. Tanis was pleased in my thoughts concerning the inspirational sermon he preached on. It is always in my best love in Christ to give my honest opinions when asked.

Well, I hope that God conclude a lot to his will by the things you are doing my man. In hopes that they will continue the trend for you but, that you move on to bigger and more daring things in God. So what's up with your trip overseas are you still going well, I am praying for you still concerning that there my man.

Wayne Wesbrook #999281

Source: www.tdcj.state.tx.us/index.htm 9/5/01

Date of Birth-2/1/58
Height 5'-10"
Weight-296 lbs.
Prior Prison Record-None

Summary of incident:
    On November 13, 1997, in Channelview, Wesbrook was invited over to the residence of his ex-wife, a 32-year-old white female. Wesbrook believed this meeting was for a possible marital reconciliation, but when he arrived, there were others present. He sat around drinking with all of them. At some point in the evening, Wesbrook noticed that his ex-wife and two of the men had slipped away, and when he went into the bedroom, he found her having sex with both of the men. Wesbrook then went to his truck and pulled out hid .36-caliber rifle and returned to the residence. He then fatally shot his ex-wife and all three of the males in the residence. Another female was injured, but survived the shooting.
Source: www.tdcj.state.tx.us 9/5/01

Greetings Mike,   May 30, 2000
    Well I received your letter at mail call this afternoon and it was most welcomed. As for my soul, I have asked the Lord assistance everyday since June of 1998. My trial was on June 15th and I was convicted June 23rd with 13 jurors instead of the traditional 12 so isn't that just wonderful.

General Colin Powel has said it best that these people in Texas are killing folks just for the sake of killing people and that man knows a kill when he sees it don't you think? The days before my trial I had myself moved to a special unit inside the jail so not to be bothered with snitches.

In April of 96 I was in NY on my way to CT. I was going to Norwich that's where my wives family is from and they still live there. They are all a bunch of looney alcoholics and drink too much all the time. They love to raise the roof and make trouble for one another. I stayed there for 5 days and then I left because I couldn't stand them anymore. My wives mother threatened to have me killed because she didn't like my looks. I tell you, they are all looney.

Before I came to prison I was a supporter of the Death penalty but never really knew about it. Now that I am here I understand why people are trying to stop it. As for being saved, I got saved back in 1978. I am a believer and there is nothing else for me to believe in here because I know I am doomed and gurney bound.

Where I am the door may close and never let me out but when I die there's a new door that will open and there will be no more suffering and no more sorrow and it will all be great there. I have friends and family waiting on me there now! These people here in this prison may take my drab old life away from me but they cant kill my soul. I will go on living whether they like it or not. They might think they are ridding the world of another killer. Sorry to disappoint them but I will be living on the streets of gold and a land of milk and honey Praise the Lord!

People don't know what suffering is until they come here to this place and its conditions. There is no where I would rather be then at my home with my daughter of 12 years.

I have no money and times are hard here. I was given this typewriter by another inmate that was laid to rest a couple years ago. Just days after I got here to Death Row this came to me as a hand me down, as I am dyslexic and write backwards, it helps me et by. We aren't allowed to watch TV anymore and I don't know why. All we have is the radio to listen to and I have no newspaper to read. I am dumb as dirt when it comes to legal stuff so I know I where I am heading no doubt!

But my mind is strong spiritually. I have friends and chaplains that come up and check on me and help me. I also write other prisoners in other states that are on Death Row. I lost my friend earlier this month out or Arkansas. Her name was Christina Marie Riggs. We swapped scriptures and now I don't have anyone to swap with and or help me read and comprehend the Word of God. It's hard to find someone to replace the friendship I had in Christy. She was funny and yet she was sad and she wanted to die. She knew she had sinned and admitted it to the court and they wanted to kill her for it. But she was ready and I supported her all the way with her decision. I got her last letter to me; it was a poem that was lovely and moving. I have tacked it to my wall and when I think of her and the kids I read it.

Here at the Terrell Unit its full of solitude and we all live in one man cells and cant speak to our neighbors at all. All there is to do here is to wait and see for your number to come up and that is it. We are allowed one visit a week if someone can get here. The food is lousy and it is cold all the time. Some times it is even soured and that's hard to swallow but either you eat it or starve, one or the other. You don't have to be tough to survive here and you don't have to be bad, you just need to stick to yourself and respect others space and that's about it.

One doesn't have enough friends in this world as it is and I intend to have plenty before I leave on my great journey into the other side. So this is Wayne and in Waynes World we just keep on groovin dudes or dudets.

Sincerely Wayne Wesbrook #999281

Dear Friend Michael,   June 11, 2000

Please note the time it's taken me to write this letter due to my impairment. I started at 5:00p.m and now it is 5:00a.m. It has taken me 12 hours to do this. I had to watch every letter to make sure it was made right. Now you have a hand crafter letter from me that took a lot of time and care to write to you. I hate the psyche drugs they have me on because they make me sleepy and interrupt my work a lot. Its just something I have to endure to keep my sanity here.

Prison officials don't like the world to know about what's going on in this Hell Hole. It's not hot here like in most prisons. Here we have a chilled air system so it's a/c here all year round with no heat. The food is bad here, most of the time it's cold to lukewarm. People don't believe the conditions we have to exist in here. We are enclosed in a solid steel cell with tap water from our toilet, which is also our sink. The lighting is fluorescent indirect lighting. There is a window 3 feet high and 4 inches wide and mine faces due north. I can see the sun set as I have a westerly view also. I watch the sun set a lot. I figure I better get as much of that in as I can because before long they will be taking me to the death house. The acoustics are bad here. It echoes outside like you are in a steel tunnel so it is hard to hear sometimes. 84 men in a section and mix in mental health with that and many just go insane inside their cells.

Suicide is a regular thing here. We don't have a lot to do inside the cells. We can sleep or exercise with push-ups or sit-ups. Me at a whopping 400lbs. I sleep a lot. I weighed 279lbs when I was arrested and with nothing to do, well you know, you gain easy. I am not proud of my weight but it's mainly due to my nervous habits. It's sometimes hard to survive in here.

The prison guards seem to be 90% women and 10% men. The Death Row guards are mostly ugly old hags. Some are abused women looking for revenge on us men and we get a lot of Hell out of them. And then there are the ones that like to come up to us and tease us. A lot are black and lippy and like to be the boss.

My case is a sudden passion case. It is capital due to the fact more then 2 were killed. I mean how would you feel if you were baited and trapped and people tried to abuse you. The whole time trying to push me to my limits. No one knows what went on or what the truth is. There were no witnesses that can say they seen or heard anything. He anything anyone seen was me putting a rifle in my truck. No one knows what really happened but me. The psychologist at my trial pointed out there are many things wrong with me. I have all the proof that needs to be offered. This was a case of sudden passion plain and simple. I need help but I can't afford $300,000 and the attorneys. There is no justice in Texas.

I am curious but would you be able to help me out by sending a cross-reference Bible to me? I haven't written this much since I got here. My biggest problem here is sleep. The guards slam the iron gates and steel doors and when you do go to sleep they want you to give them a verbal response with your name and number. The government placed a new law in effect, if you through urine or feces at a guard it's a class 3 felony. Boy like that's gonna stop a Death Row inmate!

My background is not botched by crime sprees. I was a hard working and caring person and this is what I get when I make a mistake in life? You lose your life and people tell lies about you. I don't get it! The state would say I planned to kill all 5 people. Not so! All these people were capable of killing me. They all had records and wrap sheets and me I had not one. But now they see me as trouble. Here I am, a volunteer fireman who goes around helping people and I get in trouble one time and its time to kill me I'm dangerous? The people really didn't look into my case. The jury was more worried about being put up in a motel if they didn't give me the Death penalty. Now in September it'll be 3 years since I been locked up.

I have endured a lot here and learned a lot too. I learned about freedom and what it is to be free. I learned to stay away from trouble, for prison is a stock full of trouble at every turn. You have to watch all your P's and Q's here or you could die before your time. All I want is to go home and go back to work as a truck driver and make a living. I want to raise my daughter. She is about to turn 13 years old and she needs me. I need her too but if Texas has their way they will kill me here soon.

Well I'll close for now. Your friend Wayne #999281

Hello again Michael,   July 6, 2000

I hope things are well in your life. As for my daughter Sunny, she was just here about an hour ago. This was her second visit here. She is staying with my parents right now. Her mom wasn't the lady involved in the case. She is very much alive and very well. I suppose it was Sunny's step-dad that molested her and that's why she was living with me at the time of this incident. But the night of the killing she was spending it over my parents' house. But she is in good hands and she's doing well as can be expected under the circumstances.

Thank you for the Bible I got this last Saturday. It came as a surprise to me but then I seen it came from you. This is exactly what I wanted. I have already been in the Word 3 times today. There is a calm over me since I started reading it. You have blessed me, thank you so much for the gift. And the big print is easy on my eyes. Finally I don't have to strain to see. This is like a box of candy to me and I very eager to dig deeper into the word later. The references are fantastic. I really love this Bible, you don't know what it has done or meant to have this. I am overwhelmed with joy. I have the mightiest of all weapons, The Word of the Lord. I will cherish this for eternity. I wrote my folks and told them already about my gift. I doubt they will believe me but I will carry it to visitation and show them when they come. I truly feel great about getting this from you. I have asked so many people for a Bible and no one ever bothers to send me one. I have a paperback New Testament here but the print is so small my eyes cant focus very well. But I got that beat now, thank you so very much.

Have you ever heard of Frontal Lobe Lobotomy? This is a type of brain damage I have. When I get excited I can't think clearly and my mind draws a blank and I freeze or just babble along until the glitch goes away. I want to be normal like everyone else but sometimes it gets me down. I write to you for practice. I used to not be able to write as good as I do now.

I used to work as a body guard for southwestern concerts. I have had opportunities to work for entertainers like George Straight, Stevie Nix, Van Halen and others. The pay wasn't all that and the hours were lousy. You had to be on tour forever. I tried it all for a while but I got burned out. I like truck driving way more. The pay ain't super but its ok with me. I miss it a lot the highway was my life.

Well let me close for now, hope to hear from you soon- Wayne

Hey Mike,   July 25, 2000

Hi, how are you? I figure I got about 3 more years on this planet before I go meet our Father in Heaven. I am not scared of dying because the Lord has shown me where I will live and what is in store for me. I live for my day of death to meet Jesus. There is a lot of false religions here. There are 3 sun worshippers here on this pod with me and they cant stand the fact that I have had a change of heart to the way that think. Some of the guards think it is wonderful that I speak about the Lord, they even bring me material from their church and I read it. Both of my parents think I have turned into a Jesus freak and I guess you could say I have. I found a program on the radio that I like and listen to a lot of scriptures read from it. You spoke of Orien Joiner but I didn't know him I had just heard of him. I have a friend that is a preacher in La and knew Orien. We have a lot of good people here that are trying to save souls but most turn their head to it. They aren't ready yet to devote their lives to the Lord. If they only knew what they were passing by or doing they wouldn't be believing in their fake sun god. Well let me close, I feel I need to pray for a while. Take care and thank you once again for the bible it means the world to me you just don't know.

Your brother in Christ Wayne Wesbrook "AKA the Bigun"

Dear Mike,   Aug 13, 2000

My neighbor is getting kind of jealous of me because I have so many friends that write me and talk to me about the Lord. I have an inkling that he wants to get saved before they execute him. His case is in federal court right now and it is just a matter of time until he gets affirmed and gets a date. His name is Robert Tennard; you might write him and just get his tone on his faith status and see what he says to you. His number is 000860. Just check him out. He's a black dude but he gets along with all the white people here that I can see and he too can use a person to write to.

    Your brother in the fight against Satan- Wayne

Hey Michael what's new,   Sept. 02, 2000

    I just got your letter and was surprised to hear from you again. I figured that you might have gotten bored with me and decided to find a new person to write to. I am going to send you a packet of some people that you and your friends can write. One of these guys is pretty cool. Me and him were celled next to one another at the Ellis unit. He has a kid that is kind of following in his footsteps you could say. His name is Roy Pippin. When or if anyone writes him, go easy with the questions at first. He'll want to get to know who you are first before detailing out his story to you. There is a profile of each person's crime on the sheets but don't take it for truth. TDCJ will write anything about a person just to make them look as bad as possible. You had asked a question regarding my daughter. Mike, I look at it this way. She's 13 now and by the time they kill me she will be from 16-20 years old and understand more by that time. If she wants to come I will put her on the list. We trust one another and don't lie to one another. When things aren't going well there at home she writes me and asks for my opinion on things. She has been raised around grownups and she acts like one. If you met her you wouldn't think she is 13 years old. She doesn't have a lot of friends but she does have trouble with school, mainly math, like I did. She is in 6th grade and doing algebra already!

    Breakfast here is served at 3 in the morning. We eat a lot of pancakes and not near as many eggs, as we should. Breakfast is usually like pancakes hash browns and 1 pint of 1% milk and some Cheerios, either frosted or regular. The next meal is lunch and is served about 10a.m. Lunch might be anything but their Mexican food is what I really like. I like the baked chicken and the meatloaf too but the servings are small. It is like the size of a small pocket calculator and it is just not enough. You are only allowed one tray so you could starve easy if it weren't for the extra stuff you could buy from the commissary.

    Texas just killed Gary Graham. Gary was a bad dude in his hood true enough but get this. They say it was a robbery and a killing by Gary.

The dead guy had $6,000 on him when they found his body and another thing is that the weapon that was used, the supposedly found it. But the ballistics show that the bullets from the recovered weapon and the bullets in the body don't match up. Yet they used this evidence to convict Gary. It is pretty simple that they messed up and they were covering up. Janet Reno is now looking into the Graham case and found out that the prosecution was holding back evidence that could have saved Gary. They just killed an innocent black man and there was no doubt about it.

Your friend until the end. Wayne

P.S. What I miss most since I have been locked up. You know that Sunday is my anniversary. That's the day I came to prison for the 1st time. September 3rd, 1998.

Well what I miss the most is sitting outside my home under the shade of the trees listening to the radio while watching my pet squirrels play and chase each other. I used to feed them pecans pre-shelled, they loved them. They would see me outside and come running. I had a tray that I would fill up with pecans and they would sit and eat off of it. I bought some dried corn feeders and they would climb up and eat the corn too. I finally named them all. One was sally and one was Scooter. I could barely tell them apart but I knew old Sally. She would come up real close and eat by me. She had a bunch of little babies and boy we were in squirrel Heaven. There was like 14 or 15 of them at a time. My daughter says they don't come around anymore because I'm not there feeding them and I miss that a lot.

I miss working and driving and going fishing. Funny I had a summer place not ten miles from where this unit is. I sold it about a month ago, the lot and the mobile home. It was needing attention. I sold it all for $10,000. I put my rig up for sale for $75,000. That trailer and cooler rig is also a bargain that someone will get.

I miss it all. I miss seeing my daughter and giving her a hug now and then. I miss barbecuing. I loved to cook outside and I had this pit that I bought. It was made for brisket. I would cook up some meals out of this world on that thing. It was like 5 feet long and man it would cook. I'd go buy a cord of wood and then cook right under those same shady trees. The funny thing is people love to come over when you are barbecuing. I miss the freedom of coming and going when I want.

I miss my friends. I miss going to church and I miss seeing my Pastor but that will never happen again because he passed away last year.

See there is so many things I miss. There isn't just one thing. Just being home would be a dream come true to me. If there was any one thing

it would be to be back at home with my family. That would be a blessing to me. I want to tend the yard and get it back in shape and just do the every day stuff. That is what I miss as of right now.
      Later brother. Wayne

Hey Mike,   Sept 16, 2000
      They been calling me the preacher man around here on this pod. I like that it shows that I got their attention and that's good. There are even some here that come to me and ask me questions about the Bible so I know the Lord is working with me here and I'm not alone.
      Say does your campus at college have benches to sit on and stuff? Do you ever just sit out and look at the stars at night and wonder about them? Do you ever just sit and think about how amazing it is that earth we are on never falls apart. Do you ever just wish that the Lord would just come and take us home? I think of these things all the time.
      About my wife... I got tired of her games and wanted to leave the house that night of the incident. Then I ended up exchanging words with a so-called friend I knew as a car thief and a dope dealer. He ends up stealing my keys and runs back into the apartment. I don't know what is about to happen to me if I go back in there. I have a rifle in my truck and when I go back inside to meet these people, all they have on their minds is to harm me. I have my 30.06 deer rifle in my hand and they start threatening to kill me. One of them charges me and another sprays a beer in my face and the gun goes off. Another one tries to attack me and he gets shot also. I am like totally out of my mind now and humiliated that these people tried to kill me. I go into the bedroom and find my wife in bed with this dude. This sends me over the edge and I try to shoot at him. My wife was moving out of the way and she catches a slug. I shoot again and the guy goes down. I didn't even realize that my wife was hit until I turned on the light. When I went outside there were people screaming at me. I lost all my train of thought and couldn't think right. I remember it all like it was yesterday. I see this in my head everyday and cry and have wishes that I was like them. Just to be dead would answer all my wishes. You don't know Mike how many nights I have nightmares and bad thoughts of trying to kill myself and all of the struggles I go through. I worship God everyday and pray constantly for Gods help in these areas. To this very day I wish there was a way to turn back the clock so none of this would of ever happened. Love will do many things to a man and beer will too. It only adds to your hurt and you want the pain to go away but it

is always there. My thinking wasn't right that night and it effected my life in the long run. I put trouble in paradise I guess you could say. 5 people shot and killed in one night.

See ya   Wayne

Hey Mike,   October 25, 2000

It's always a pleasure to hear from you and your roommates up there at college. Your friendship means the world to me. I thank you so much for bothering to care for me and pray for me.

As for right now my father is in the hospital for his lung cancer. They removed ¼ of his lower lung and he is coughing up a lot of blood. If you don't mind please pray that he makes a quick recovery and the Lord take away some of his pain. He is also having some trouble with is kidneys but they aren't too bad. They even had to open up his heart and fix an artery. They said his heart is so damaged that he may need a transplant to keep him alive. I guess he is living on borrowed time now. He knows the truth of Christ and he knows he has to give in to the Lord and accept him as his personal Savior to make it to Heaven. Before the operation he was going to church and he knows what he needs to do. I pray that he gets saved before the Lord calls him home or else he will spend eternity in Hell. We all have fallen short of the Lord and he died for all of us. He died for all our sins and no matter how big or little they are, if a person doesn't get saved then they are going to have to face the music one of these days.

We got to stick together as brothers in Christ and win as many souls as we can and turn their eyes to the Lord. There seem to be so many that want to believe but never do. They just can't lend themselves to accept the Word of God as truth and put away their sins.

I just got my medication delivered for the day. I take some blood pressure medication. I used to have normal blood pressure until I came here and started gaining weight. These cells aren't big enough to run in except in place and to do a lot of sit ups and pull-ups and stuff. I am just not the type to do exercises and stuff. I do like to play volleyball but that is near impossible here since we have single man recreation time. No TV's, no telling what they will take away next. They took our finger nail clippers away just a few months ago. They told us that they became a security risk. What a joke that was. This place is a joke to start with. These people are terrified of us and you can see it every time they take you out of your cell and if you move too fast for them, that truly scares them. They carry big batons to wail you with if you get radical. I don't think they know how to use them properly. I had a stick training course and am certified in the field of protecting myself.

Well I hope to hear from you again real soon. Take care and tell the others I say hello and I will pray for you and them as I always do.

Well brother take it easy and try to get some A's and I will be here waiting to hear from you soon.

     Waiting for the Lords return- Wayne

Hello Mike,   Dec. 14, 2000

What's up? Not much here. I'm just looking for the holidays to end soon. Christmas is around the corner and all of us here are more less depressed around this time. My dad isn't doing much better these days and that's about it.

It's been the same old stuff around here. There was an escape down in Beeville Texas. Seven got out and are on the run somewhere. I heard they got some guns and because of their lack of security they got out. I was told by one of the guys here that two of them were spending life terms for murder but now they are on the loose. It just makes us all look bad that's all it does. It always comes back on us here.

  That's all for now bro.   Wayne

Hey Mike,   Jan. 10, 2001

From the Terrell Prison unit…It is good to hear from you again. I am happy to say that James Tennard has a friend of yours he is writing with too.

The escapees are still on the run. Rumors fly that they killed a man and robbed a store and may have split up. The media is always messed up with the facts.

I have been speaking a lot lately to the men here about getting saved. I have a giant burden on my shoulders for them and their souls. I throw out some crumbs of Bible to them and if they are hungry for more I persist. Satan will throw obstacles in your way like everything from football on the radio to anything. All in the way of winning souls. All distractions but God can overcome them.

By the way we have been on lock down since the third. I hope we come off of it by the 12th. I need to restock from the commissary badly. The meals have been really bitter lately. I won't starve but I need something with flavor to it. Take care for now and pray for the escapees and me.

    Many blessings- Wayne

Hey Mike,   Jan. 23, 2001

    What's cooking there? Noting much here. Our seven desperados are still on the loose. The media has pt so much scary stuff into their eyes I bet they are hiding in deep cover right now. They are making them look like a modern day bunch of Bonnie and Clyde's.

    My father is home from the hospital finally. He is really weak now. Before he came home to my mother's house there was a fire there. Sunny was lighting a candle with a match and thought the match was out but it wasn't when she threw it into the trashcan besides the bed. It caught fire and the bed and carpet were ruined. The whole room is smoke damaged. I don't know how much the insurance is going to cover. The bed was electric where you can raise the head and feet by remote. It was new and it cost like $3,000. At least my father was not there at the time. His lungs are real sensitive to things in the air. When it rains it pours at my moms house.

    Well, I took off a few days to write the rest of this but now they c7aught 4 of the 7 escapees. I guess we will be seeing them here soon. One committed suicide. I can't say I blame him. They would have just executed him soon enough. The rest will get the needle now too. Two are still on the lamb according to the news. Hey have you ever wrote Angel Resindez? They call him the Choo-Choo man in here. He is the railroad killer. I hear is kind of a spiritual person now, what ever that may mean.

    Take care and I'll be praying for you-Your Big Bro. Wayne

Hello Michael,   Jan. 27, 2001

    How are you doing this day? When you mentioned Mr. Perez I had an idea. Maybe I should make a gesture and let the state kill me on closed circuit TV. I think it is time to show the public what they are missing and how it really goes when they start pumping the juice of joy through your veins.

    I know that by the time you get this letter you will know that all seven have been captured and one is dead. I figured something like that would happen. I am more surprised that there wasn't a battle royal between them and the cops. We were all expecting a big show down I think.

You know what is ironic. We all have freedom of speech but I have no one to talk too and we all have freedom of the press but I can't ever get it to read it. They treat us like rabid dogs here. We aren't animals, we are humans too. We need help too! I am sorry to get on a soapbox but it is so true.

Be careful on your trip to Africa my brother. There are like wars and such going on over there. Take care and may the Lord bless you now and always.

Your bud in Texas D/R Wayne

Hello Mike, March 19, 2001

I am glad to hear from you again. We are on lock down here. They lock us down a lot. This time it's over a pry bar that came up missing. The warden is threatening to keep us locked down until someone coughs it up. That can be like 90 days!

My dad is in serious trouble. He is near death according to my mother. Sunny came here for a visit last Tuesday. Mom was pretty upset over dad. She doesn't know what to do about him. There is really nothing she can do about it. Pray for him ok.

Wayne

Greeting Mike, May 2001

Hope this finds you in the best of spirits. There was a bill passed in Texas stating that they be no longer executing the retarded here. I know it's been a long time since I wrote you but it's been hectic here.

There was a stabbing on the unit yesterday. They say it wasn't gang related but that is a crock. Unless you are on Death Row, you are probably in a gang. This place is a gladiator farm for a bunch of young punks. It ain't made for an old man like myself.

Well I am going to go for now. I will pray for while you are in Kenya. See ya.

Sincerely, Wayne

Jordan Crystal

(The name of this inmate, and locations, were changed to protect the innocent)

Dear Mike, 5-7-01

Greetings my brother in Jesus' name. I truly enjoyed your witnessing letter but my friend you are 42 years late. I accepted Christ as my personal Savior when I was 12 and he is my best friend now. Actually it won't be 42 years until my birthday on July 22nd. I openly admit that I am a sinner and know that I am guaranteed a place in Heaven through the promises that Christ made.

Here in Waynesburg, Pa I am in the L-5 building with 128 other men on Death Row. 85% of them are either Muslim, atheist or some other belief. Its difficult to do much witnessing here since we are in our cells 23 hours a day and 24 hours a day on the weekends. There are 4 pods in a building and 32 cells per pod. 16 downstairs and 16 upstairs. I am upstairs and out of the 16 cells up here with me there are 7 Christians and 1 atheist and 8 Muslims.

I am happy to be saved. I know I am still a sinner but I am forgiven. I am a soon to be 55 year old white guy. I have grey hair and hazel blue eyes. I stand at 6'-1" tall and weigh 220lbs. I love the Lord with a burning that is beyond words. I write poetry mostly about God and to my ladylove. I am a former U.S. Marine who has done 3 tours of duty in Vietnam. I was also at one time a Washington D.C. firefighter/paramedic. I was even used on the presidential security team. I can fly almost anything that has wings on it. I have been on Death Row for 20 years now. It will be 21 years on July 4th. I've been married two times and have four daughters. They each want nothing to do with me.

I will get going now. God Bless.
                Jordan

Dear Mike, 5-18-01

It is good to hear from you my friend. Enclosed in this letter is a sheet I drew up for you to help you picture my cell, pod, building and yard. Remember though, I am not an artist. This is a Super Max prison and there are two blocks that house capital sentenced inmates. "G" block (96 cells) and "L" block (128 cells). Philadelphia (Graterford) has the rest. Pittsburgh used to but in 1995 they transferred us down here. "L" block was just built 3 years ago and I was one of the 1st moved over here.

A year ago they built a kitchen next door so our food would be hot. Ha ha- it hasn't been hot yet!

Since 1995 I have lost 3 buddies to execution and the state. Right now I am stuck in the 3rd circuit court of appeals.

When I joined the Marines in 1965 I was a "Boot". Then a Marine never ever called a Marine a soldier. It's a pride thing and on top of that we are supposed to be better then an army soldier. I was in some very violent and hairy firefights against the Vietcong and the NVA (North Vietnamese Army). I had lost a lot of buddies in Vietnam. As to how many of the opposition that I have killed…that is hard to say. I have been in full attacks by the V.C. and NVA where 1100 bodies were supposedly counted. I can say that without a doubt I killed 15 and 6 of them were in hand to hand combat with a knife. I was an E-5 Sgt. The 1st fire fight I was in I was so scared I wet my pants. Later I became a platoon sergeant and we'd go to a position to wait for any pilot who needed to bail out. Then he'd head for us and we'd try to get to him before the V.C. did. We would take him to a land zone and then carry him by chopper back to base. I did 3 tours over there and spent the last 30 days I had on barracks restriction.

After I went to prison I slowly gave myself back to Gods will. It was right after I got my stay of execution that the United States began bombing Iraq. I saw a thing on television about writing to a serviceman over there and it gave the address. I addressed it "to any Marine". A young man wrote me and we became close. I urged him to make a career out of the army but he wanted to go to college. (He graduated New York University 2 years ago). He gave me his home address and I was doing some origami artwork and wanted to send him mom some of it. I made a 1 ½ inch deep box and put a flowering tree magazine picture for the background. I had been writing to Jeff for almost a year and a half at his home some my letters weren't unusual. I made a paper tree with paper leaves and wrote a prayer on it. I sent it to his mom. She was so thrilled because she wanted an excuse to write me and speak to me but she didn't have one. She wrote a thank you note and asked if I'd mind if she wrote me. When I got mail a few days later and I saw the guard with a letter in his hand and the name Laurie was on the return address I became like a little schoolboy. I danced around my cell and so much joy arose I began giggling and wanted to yell but didn't.

I learned God only gives his best to his children. Be patient.

Hey be careful on your trip to Africa. Americans are targets for kidnappings over there and Christians get killed a lot over there. Go with

God by your side and don't go getting in trouble so I will have to break out of here and rescue you. I'll give you the same advice I gave to Jeff before Desert Storm. Be aware of what is going on around you at all times and be alert as to who is approaching you. Listen to God. He'll let you know when things just don't feel right. I will be praying for your safety.

    Child of the King,
        Jordan

John Burks

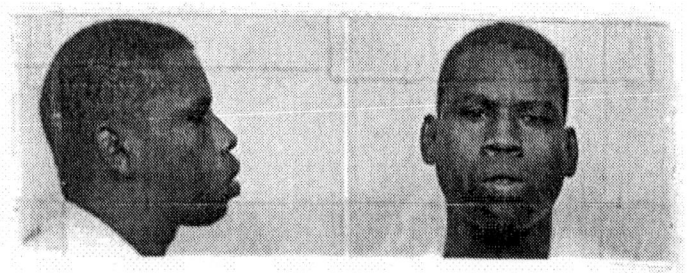

Source: www.tdcj.state.tx.us/index.htm 9/5/01

Burks was convicted in the 1989 murder of Jesse Contreras during the armed robbery of Jesse's Tortilla Factory in Waco Texas. Contreras was shot in the mouth and the chest with a .25- Caliber pistol during the robbery.

Date of Execution: June 14, 2000

Burks didn't seem to care either way. No indication of ever claiming a religion he went out of this world cheering on his favorite football team and asking people to pray for him. Perhaps he never even thought there was a God. Maybe he was just trying to get his mind off of what was to come. The fact is we don't know, but what we do know is, Burks was about to meet God and he would either be his Judge or his Savior. It all depended on Burks and if he had ever accepted Jesus Christ as his Lord and Savior, before he entered eternity.

Last Statement:

Hey, how are y'all doing? Alright, it's gong to be alright. There's some guys I didn't get a chance to visit with, ah I met when I first drove up here...Lester Byers, Chris Black, Alba, John Alba, and Rosales Rock. You know who you are. The Raiders are going all the way, y'all (mumbles...Mo-B). Y'all pray for me. And it's going to be alright. That's it and it's time to roll up out of her. It's going down, let's get it over with. That's it.

Source: www.tdcj.state.tx.us 9/5/01

David Goff

Goff was convicted in the murder of 34-year-old Michael McGuire. McGuire was shot to death during an attempted robbery. The victim was reportedly kidnapped upon leaving a drug rehab center in Fort Worth and was shot after being handcuffed and drugged. Source: www.tdcj.state.tx.us/index.htm 9/5/01

Mike,   1-28-01 (Sunday)

Hello! Sorry that I am only now writing you back. I have a had a lot of stuff on my mind. And now that I do have I time I come bearing some news. I have been set an execution date for April 25th. It was not the thing that I wanted to hear from them. Though this is the only execution date that I have had. It is likely to be the only one. It is up to God to allow it to go through or to stop it. I understand that God is the one who can allow me to live or die. I also know that I have eternal life with Christ that no one can take.

I will admit that I have felt this sour pit inside of me since Friday when I learned of the date. It is like a weight has settled within my body and is taking what strength I have. I pray that God gives me the strength to overcome this. But for the most part I am doing well. God has given me much peace already. At every stage of the process there has been that moment when I have had to stop and allow God to take me back down that path that I have been. The path of the cross. It is a way for me to be reminded that I have made a commitment that God will be my strength. I then read Psalm 3. "LORD, how are they increased that trouble me! Many are they that rise up against me. Many there be which say of my soul, There is no help for him in God. Selah. But thou, O LORD, art a shield for me; my glory, and the lifter up of mine head. I cried unto the LORD with my voice, and he heard me out of his holy hill. Selah. I laid me down and slept; I awaked; for the LORD sustained me. I will not be afraid of ten thousands of people, that have set themselves against me round about. Arise, O LORD; save me, O my God: for thou hast smitten all mine enemies upon the cheek bone; thou hast broken the teeth of the ungodly. Salvation belongeth unto the LORD: thy blessing is upon thy people. Selah."

Take care and I will keep you in prayer. Just pray for me that God's will is done and above all things His love is shown no matter what.
      David

Date of Execution: April 25, 2001
Last meal: None requested.
Last Statement:

I want to give all the praise to God and glory and thank him for all that he done for me. With this let all debts be paid that I owed - real or imagined. The slate is wiped clean; all marks erased other than that there is no justice. That's not justice. Praise the Lord. Glory to Jesus Christ. Praise the Lord God.

Source: www.tdcj.state.tx.us 9/5/01

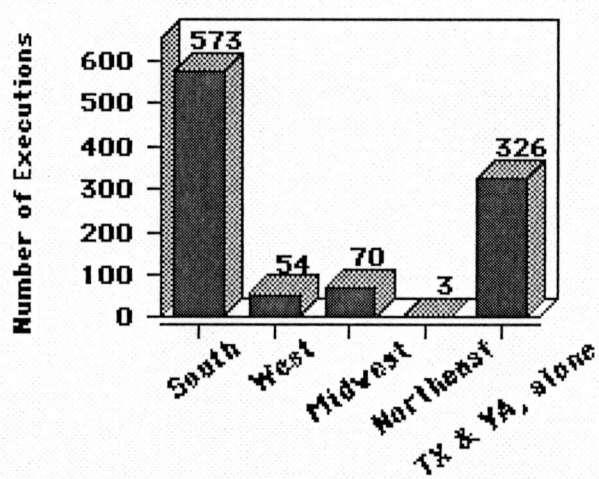

(Chart provided by Death Penalty Information Center)

-Texas carried out the 700th United States execution since the reinstatement of the Death penalty in 1976. The March 7th execution of Dennis Dowthitt in Texas was the 700th. Over 80% of those executions occurred in the south, and 326 of the 700 (46%) were carried out in Texas and Virginia alone.

Calvin McGee #999298

On October 1st 1997, during the nighttime hours, McGee and his co-defendants murdered a 61-year-old black female during the course of a robbery at a Kentucky Fried Chicken restaurant in Houston, Texas. McGee and her co-defendants were trying to rob her of her 1998 Cadillac while she was at the drive through of this restaurant. McGee and the co-defendants pulled in line behind the victim's car. McGee and one of his friends got out of their vehicle and ordered the victim at gunpoint to get into the back of her car. The victim got out of the car and screamed at which time McGee shot her once in the head with a .38-caliber pistol.

Source: www.tdcj.state.tx.us 9/5/01

Dear Mike,   Saturday June 24th, 2000

I hope and pray that when this letter reaches you it will find you in the best of health and the highest of spirits.

Thank you for those strengthening words you sent and the power behind them. And to answer your question, yes I am saved.

I sincerely asked Christ to come into my life back on 10/8/97. And everything you are saying is true. I am 23 years old and I've been here on Death Row for 15 months now. I am not upset, worried or afraid. God is the one who allowed me to be sentenced to death. It hurts me a lot to know that I am responsible for the death of another human's life, even though it was an accident.

But that is another subject in itself. Another reason I am not afraid or worried is because I am able to focus on Him day and night. I don't worry about my appeal and this flesh that I am occupying right now. Let me put it like this. Matthew says, 10:37-40 "He that loveth father or mother more than me is not worthy of me: and he that loveth son or daughter more than me is not worthy of me. And he that taketh not his cross, and followeth after me, is not worthy of me. He that findeth his life shall lose it: and he that loseth his life for my sake shall find it. He that receiveth you receiveth me, and he that receiveth me receiveth him that sent me." I focus on this every day. I love my daughter and my mom. But I am loving Christ more. He is the foundation and the center of my life.

Christ Jesus knows my heart better than anyone else and I thank Him so much for the peace He has given me.

Right now there are a lot of people going to church and living the same way they used to. They feel that church will save them. A lot of them fall under Matthew 6:1-2. They enjoy the attention so much. I used to be like that but I asked Jesus to forgive me. There is no big sin and small sin. Sin is sin. The world teaches that certain little sins will be overlooked. Christ said it is all evil and will not enter into Heaven.

Right now I want so bad to go and be with my Father, but I am His servant and wish to do His will.

I pray and hope we become pals. I always look for people to talk with on biblical subjects. I talk to some of the brothers here but I am not able to get deep into it with them because of the circumstances here. For now I will close this letter, hopefully never forever.

Your brother in Christ Jesus,
Calvin McGee

P.S. here is an illustration I heard somewhere, maybe you can use it someday.

A young man who had been raised an atheist was training to be an Olympic diver. The only religious influence in his life came from his outspoken saved friends. The young diver never really paid much attention to his friends' sermons, but he heard them often.

One night the diver went to the indoor pool at the college he attended. The lights were all off, but the pool area had huge skylights and the moon was full and bright. The young man climbed to the highest diving board and as he turned his back to the pool he stood on the edge of the board. He slowly extended his arms out and he saw his shadow on the wall. The shadow from the moonlight was in the shape of a cross.

Instead of diving he knelt down and finally asked God to come into his life, forgive him of his sins and save his soul.

As the young man stood back up maintenance man walked in and turned the lights on. The pool had been drained for repairs.

David Berkowitz

Formerly known as the Son of Sam.

David was never on Death Row but is now serving 365 years in prison for the murder of 6 people and wounding of many others. He pleaded guilty to all charges brought against him. Berkowitz is up for parole in 2002. That summer will mark the 25th year of his capture. David's story is amazing and the changes in his life are as bold as going from black to white.

"I DIDN'T WANT TO HURT THEM, I ONLY WANTED TO KILL THEM" Son of Sam

"I have asked you kindly to stop that dog from howling all day long, yet he continues to do so. I pleaded with you. I told you how this is destroying my family. We have no peace, no rest.

Now I know what kind of a person you are and what kind of a family you are. You are cruel and inconsiderate. You have no love for any other human beings. Your selfish, Mr. Carr. My life is destroyed now. I have nothing to lose anymore. I can see that there shall be no peace in my life, or my families life until I end yours."

April 17, 1977, this letter had been left at the scene of the murder.

Dear Captain Joseph Borrelli,

    I am deeply hurt by your calling me a wemon hater. I am not. But I am a monster. I am the 'Son of Sam.' I am a little brat. When father Sam gets drunk he gets mean. He beats his family. Sometimes he ties me up to the back of the house. Other times he locks me in the garage. Sam loves to drink blood. 'Go out and kill,' commands father Sam. 'Behind our house some rest. Mostly young -- raped and slaughtered -- their blood drained -- just bones now. Papa Sam keeps me locked in the attic too. I can't get out but I look out the attic window and watch the world go by. I feel like an outsider. I am on a different wavelength then everybody else -- programmed too kill. However, to stop me you must kill me. Attention all police: Shoot me first -- shoot to kill or else keep out of my way or you will die!

    Papa Sam is old now. He needs some blood to preserve his youth. He has had too many heart attacks. 'Ugh, me hoot, it hurts, sonny boy.' I miss my pretty princess most of all. She's resting in our ladies house. But I'll see her soon. I am the 'Monster' -- 'Beelzebub' -- the chubby behemouth. I love to hunt. Prowling the streets looking for fair game -- tasty meat. The women of Queens are prettyist of all. It must be the water they drink. I live for the hunt -- my life. Blood for papa. Mr. Borrelli, sir, I don't want to kill anymore.

    No sur, no more but I must, 'honour thy father.' I want to make love to the world. I love people. I don't belong on earth. Return me to yahoos. To the people of Queens, I love you. And I want to wish all of you a happy Easter. May God bless you in this life and in the next. And for now I say goodbye and goodnight.

POLICE: Let me haunt you with these words:

I'll be back! I'll be back! To be interrpreted as - bang, bang, bang, bang - ugh!!

Yours in murder Mr. Monster.

April 30, 1977

Hello from the cracks in the sidewalks of NYC and from the ants that dwell in these cracks and feed in the dried blood of the dead that has settled into the cracks.

Hello from the gutters of NYC, which is filled with dog manure, vomit, stale wine, urine, and blood. Hello from the sewers of NYC which swallow up these delicacies when they are washed away by the sweeper trucks.

Don't think because you haven't heard [from me] for a while that I went to sleep. No, rather, I am still here. Like a spirit roaming the night. Thirsty, hungry, seldom stopping to rest; anxious to please Sam.

Sam's a thirsty lad. He won't let me stop killing until he gets his fill of blood. Tell me, Jim, what will you have for July 29? You can forget about me if you like because I don't care for publicity. However, you must not forget Donna Lauria and you cannot let the people forget her either. She was a very sweet girl.

Not knowing what the future holds, I shall say farewell and I will see you at the next job? Or should I say you will see my handiwork at the next job? Remember Ms. Lauria. Thank you.

Here are some names to help you along. Forward them to the Inspector for use by the NCIC [National Crime Information Center] Center. They have everything on computer, everything. They just might turn up, from some other crimes. Maybe they could make associations.

Duke of Death. Wicked King Wicker. The twenty-two Disciples of Hell. And lastly, John Wheaties, rapist and suffocator of young girls. P.S.,PS : J.B please inform all the detectives working the slayings to remain. Drive on, think positive, get off your butts, knock on coffins, etc.

In their blood and from the gutter-- 'Sam's creation' .44

June 10, 1977

Dear Jack, I'm sorry to hear about that fall you took from the roof of your house. Just want to say 'I'm sorry' but I'm sure it won't be long until you feel much better, healthy, well and strong: Please be careful next time. Since your going to be confined for a long time, let us know if Nann needs anything.

Sincerely: Sam and Francis

Sam Carr, who owned the barking dog, supported this idea. Sam had a son named John 'Wheaties' Carr , who Berkowitz mentioned in one of his letters as one of the demons masters. Carr committed suicide in the late 70's. The number '666' was sliced on Carr's hand and next to his lifeless body, written in blood, were the letters S.S.N.Y.C., an acronym that was said to mean 'Son of Sam, New York City'.

The Berkowitz Timeline to Terror

July 29, 1976- Donna Lauria who was 18 years old and Jody Valente who was 19, were shot when David Berkowitz walked up to their car and pulled a .44 Calibur hand gun from his paper bag and emptied the gun into their car. Lauria was killed but Valente survived the attack. Maury Terry's research concluded that, "Donna raised her right arm as the bullets shattered the closed passenger's window. One of the slugs entered above her right elbow, traveled downward through her forearm, exited beneath her wrist, entered her back and killed her instantly".

October 23, 1976- Rosemary Keenan, 18, and Carl Denaro, 20, sat in a parked car when Berkowitz walked up to the car and proceeded to shoot the .44 handgun. The bullets, somehow never hit Keenan, while Denaro was hit once in the head and survived the attack.

November 27, 1976- Donna DeMasi, 16, and Joanne Lomino, 18, were returning to their home. On Lomino's doorstep Berkowitz came up to them ladies and began shooting. Both Joanne and Donna were hit. Although Donna escaped with a recoverable wound, Joanne was permanently paralyzed.

January 30 1977- Christine Freund, 26, and John Diel, 30, sat in a parked car. Berkowitz watched the two from behind a tree. Berkowitz approached the car and let off three shots into the car, then ran. John was unharmed. Christine Freund was shot once and died later that night.

March 8, 1977- Virginia Voskerichian, 19, a Russian-language major at Barnard College, was walking home from class when David walked up to her. As he raised the .44, Virginia raised her schoolbooks to cover her face. David fired one time and rushed back to his car. Virginia died instantly.

April 17 1977- Valentina Suriana, 18, and Alexander Esau, 20, became his next victims. David approached the vehicle and fired four times. Before leaving, David intentionally dropped a note addressed to Captain Joseph Borrelli on the street. Both died.

May 30, 1977- Berkowitz mailed journalist Jimmy Breslin a letter.

June 26 1977- Salvatore Lupo, 20, and Judy Placido, 17, sat in a parked car. Judy noticed a man outside the window. David opened fire. Although David fully intended to kill Judy, both she and Salvadore were only wounded. Berkowitz ran.

July 31, 1977- Bobby Violante, 20, and Stacy Moskowitz, 20, were both walking in a darkened park when they spotted a suspicious person watching them from a distance. The couple returned to their car but did not leave. Approaching the vehicle, Berkowitz shot the couple while they kissed. Bobby was hit twice in the head and survived but was permanently blinded. Stacy was hit once in the head and died later in the hospital.

August 10, 1977- It was a Wednesday night, more than a year after the first killing. David walked out of his home carrying a brown paper bag. As soon as he entered his Ford Galaxy the police surrounded him and one officer quickly placed a gun to his head ordering him to freeze.
"Now that I've got you," Falotico said, "who have I got?"
"You know," David replied
"No, I don't. You tell me." Falotico replied.
Smiling, he answered, "I'm Sam. David Berkowitz."

What David said about himself:

As far back as I can remember my childhood was not that of a normal child. It started when I was about five or six years old. I was completely uncontrollable. I would rampage through the house, sometimes overturning furniture. A tremendous force would come upon me and urge me to do destructive things to property or even to myself. Other times I would be in total silence to my parents and not respond to their outreaches of love. I would lock myself in the closet in the darkness and stay there for hours. I was depressed at times and my parents would have to pull me away from the window to keep me from committing suicide. I was a tormented child, always having psychological problems. School officials sent me to a child psychologist

It's cold and gloomy here in New York, but that's okay because the weather fits my mood -- gloomy. Dad, the world is getting dark now. I can feel it more and more. The people, they are developing a hatred for me. You wouldn't believe how much some people hate me. Many of them want to kill me. I don't even know these people, but still they hate me. Most of them are young. I walk down the street and they spit and kick at me. The girls call me ugly and they bother me the most. The guys just laugh. Anyhow, things will soon change for the better.

I'd come home to Coligni avenue like at six-thirty in the morning. It would begin then, the howling. On my days, off, I heard it all night, too. It made me scream. I used to scream out begging for the noise to stop. It never did. The demons never stopped. I couldn't sleep. I had no strength to fight. I could barely drive. Coming home from work one night, I almost killed myself in the car. I needed to sleep....The demons wouldn't give me any peace.

When I moved in the Cassaras seemed very nice and quiet. But they tricked me. They lied. I thought they were members of the human race. They weren't! Suddenly the Cassaras began to show up with the demons. They began to howl and cry out. 'Blood and death!' They called out the names of the masters! The Blood Monster, John Wheaties, General Jack Cosmo.

There was a time back in 1987, one cold winter's night, when I was in the prison yard. Another inmate walked up to me, introduced himself, and boldly told me that Jesus loved me and had a plan for my life. After he said those words I laughed at him and told him that there was no way God could love me. I told him I was too evil, that he was wasting his time. But this man had such a compassionate attitude, and I saw that he was really sincere. I cannot describe it. Let's just say he had a special glow about him. One day he offered me a small pocket New Testament which included the Psalms. He urged me to read portions of it, especially the Psalms. Some nights I would peek into the Bible just to check it out. I had never read the Bible before. I started to read the Psalms for the first time in my life, and said to myself, "My God, these are some of the most beautiful words I've ever read. I began to cry like never before. I shut my light out, got down on my knees in the darkness, and began to pour out my heart to the Lord. This was all new to me. Feelings of grief and deep remorse welled up inside. I called upon the God of Israel and talked to Him as if He were right in the cell with me. I didn't even know if God was listening. I just had to pray. And He heard my prayer.

The police and the news media used to call me 'The Son of Sam', but God has given me a new name, 'the son of hope', because now, my life is about hope.

SON OF HOPE
My Story
by David Berkowitz

May God bless everyone who is reading this message!
My name is David Berkowitz, and I am a prison inmate who has been incarcerated for more than twenty five years. I have been sentenced to prison for the rest of my life. My criminal case is well known and was called the "Son of Sam" shootings. It was eleven years ago, when I was living in a cold and lonely prison cell, that God got a hold of my life. Here is my story of Hope...

CHILD OF TORMENT

Ever since I was a small child, my life seemed to be filled with torment. I would often have seizures in which I would roll on the floor. Sometimes furniture would get knocked over. When these attacks came, it felt as if something was entering me. My mother who has long since passed away, had not control over me. I was like a wild and destructive animal. My father had to pin me to the floor until these attacks stopped. When I was in public school, I was so violent and disruptive that a teacher, who had become so angry at me, grabbed me in a headlock and threw me out of his classroom.

I was getting into a lot of fights, too. Sometimes I started screaming for no reason. And eventually my parents were ordered by school officials to take me to a child psychologist, or else I would be expelled. I had to go to this psychologist once per week for two years. Yet the therapy sessions had no affect on my behavior. During this period of my life I was also plagued with bouts of severe depression. When this feeling came over me, I would hide under my bed for hours. I would also lock myself in a closet and sit in total darkness from morning until afternoon. I had a craving for the darkness and I felt an urge to flee away from people.

A FORCE WAS AT WORK

Occasionally this same evil force would come upon me in the middle of the night. When this would happen I felt an urge to sneak out of the house and wander the dark streets. I roamed the neighborhood like an alley cat and would creep back into the house by climbing the fire escape. My parents would never know that I was gone.

I continually worried and frightened my parents because I behaved so strangely. At times I would go the entire day without talking to them. I would stay in my room talking to myself. My parents could not reach me, not even with all their love. Many times I saw them break down and cry because they saw that I was such a tormented person.

FIGHTING THOUGHTS OF SUICIDE

Thoughts of suicide often came into my mind. Sometimes I spent time sitting on a window ledge with my legs dangling over the side. We lived on the 6th floor of an old apartment building. When my dad saw me doing this he would yell at me to get back inside. I also felt powerful urges to step in front of moving cars or throw myself in front of subway trains. At times those urges were so strong that my body actually trembled. I remember that it was a tremendous struggle for me to hold on to my sanity. I had no idea what to do and neither did my parents. They had me talk to a rabbi, teachers and school counselors, but nothing worked.

MY MOTHER WAS DEAD

When I was fourteen my mother was stricken with cancer and within several months she was dead. I had no other brothers or sisters, and so it was just me and my dad. He had to work ten hours per day, six days per week. So we spent very little time together. For the most part, my mother was my source of stability. With her now gone, however, my life quickly went downhill. I was filled with anger at the loss of my mom. I felt hopeless and my periods of depression were more intense than ever. I also became even more rebellious and began to cut out of school. Yet my dad tried to help as best as he could. He managed to push me through high school. The day after I graduated I went into the Army. I had just turned 18 several weeks earlier. I joined the Army, in a sense, to start a new life and get away from my problems. But even in the service I had trouble coping, though I did manage to finish my 3 year enlistment.

THE FORCE STILL HAD ME

I got out of the service in 1974 to start life again as a civilian. All my friends that I knew before had either married or moved away. So I found myself alone and living in New York City. In 1975, however, I met some guys at a party who were, I later found out, heavily involved in the occult. I had always been fascinated with witchcraft, Satanism and occult things since I was a child. When I was growing up I watched countless horror and Satan-type movies, one of which was Rosemary's Baby. The movie in particular totally captivated my mind.

Now I was age 22 and this evil force was still reaching out to me. Everywhere I went there seemed to be a sign or a symbol pointing me to Satan. I felt as if something were trying to take control of my life. I began to read the Satanic Bible by the late Anton LaVey who founded the Church of Satan in San Francisco in1966. I began, innocently, to practice various occult rituals and incantations.

I am utterly convinced that something satanic had entered into my mind and that, looking back at all that happened, I realize that I had been slowly deceived. I did not know that bad things were going to result from all this. Yet over the months the things that were wicked no longer seemed to be such. I was headed down the road to destruction and I did not know it. Maybe I was at a point where I just didn't care.

THE HORROR BEGINS

Eventually I crossed that invisible line of no return. After years of mental torment, behavioral problems, deep inner struggles and my own rebellious ways, I became the criminal that, at the time, it seemed as if it was my destiny to become. Looking back it was all a horrible nightmare and I would do anything if I could undo everything that happened. Six people lost their lives. Many others suffered at my hand, and will continue to suffer for a lifetime. I am so sorry for that.

In 1978 I was sentenced to about 365 consecutive years, virtually burying me alive behind prison walls. When I first entered the prison system I was placed in isolation. I was then sent to a psychiatric hospital because I was declared temporarily insane. Eventually I was sent to other prisons including the infamous "Attica". As with many inmates, life in prison is a struggle. I have had my share of problems, hassles and fights. At one time I almost lost my life when another inmate cut my throat. Yet all through this - and I did not realize it until later - God had His loving hands on me.

HOPE WAS COMING

Ten years into my prison sentence and feeling despondent and without hope, another inmate came up to me one day as I was walking the prison yard on a cold winter's night. He introduced himself and began to tell me that Jesus Christ loved me and wanted to forgive me. Although I knew he meant well I mocked him because I did not think that God would ever forgive me or that He would want anything to do with me.

Still this man persisted and we became friends. His name was Rick and we would walk the yard together. Little by little he would share with me about his life and what he believed Jesus had done for him. He kept reminding me that no matter what a person did, Christ stood ready to forgive if that individual would be willing to turn from the bad things they were doing and would put their full faith and trust in Jesus Christ and what He did on the cross , dying for our sins.

He gave me a Pocket New Testament and asked me to read the Psalms. I did. Every night I would read from them. And it was at this time that the Lord was quietly melting my stone cold heart.

A NEW LIFE BEGINS

One night, I was reading Psalm 34. I came upon the 6th verse, which says, "this poor man cried, and the Lord heard him, and saved him from all his troubles". It was at that moment, in 1987, that I began to pour out my heart to God. Everything seemed to hit me at once. The guilt from what I did... the disgust at what I had become... late that night in my cold cell, I got down on my knees and I began to cry to Jesus Christ.

I told Him that I was sick and tired of doing evil. I asked Jesus to forgive me for all my sins. I spent a good while on my knees praying to Him. When I got up it felt as if a very heavy but invisible chain that had been around me for so many years was broken. A peace flooded over me. I did not understand what was happening. But in my heart I just knew that my life, somehow, was going to be different.

A DECADE OF FREEDOM

More than fifteen years have gone by since I had that first talk with the Lord. So many good things have happened in my life since. Jesus Christ has allowed me to start an outreach ministry right here in the prison where I have been given permission by prison officials to work in the "Special Needs Unit" where men who have various emotional and coping problems are housed. I can pray with them as we read our Bibles together. I get the chance to show them a lot of brotherly love and compassion.

I have worked as the Chaplain's clerk and also have a letter writing ministry. In addition, the Lord has opened ways for me to share with millions via TV programs such as Inside Edition in 1993 and A & E Investigative Reporter in 1997, what He has done in my life as well as to warn others about the dangers of getting involved in the occult.

I have also shared my testimony on several Christian TV programs such as the 700 Club in 1997, and the Coral Ridge Hour (Dr. James Kennedy) in 1999. For all these opportunities I am most thankful, and I do not feel I deserve this.

THERE'S HOPE FOR YOU TOO

One of my favorite passages of Scripture is Romans 10:13. It says, "For whosoever shall call upon the name of the Lord shall be saved." Here it is clear that God has no favorites. He rejects no one, but welcomes all who call upon Him. I know that God is a God of mercy who is willing to forgive. He is perfectly able to restore and heal our hurting and broken lives. I have discovered from the Bible that Jesus Christ died for our sins. Yet He was without sin. He took our place on that cross. He shed His blood as the full and complete payment God required for our wrong doing. The Bible also says, "For all have sinned, and come short of the glory of God". Romans 3:23. Furthermore, it says, "For the wages of sin is death; but the gift of God is eternal life through Jesus Christ our Lord". Romans 6:23. These passages make it clear that everyone has sinned. Yes, some like myself did so more than others. But all have done things wrong. Therefore, we must all make the decision to acknowledge our sins before God and be sorry for them. We need to turn from our lives of sin as well as believe that Chris was and is the Son of God.

You must believe that Jesus Christ died and was buried, and on the third day He rose again in victory, for death could not hold Him. Ask Christ to forgive you. Declare Him as Lord of your life and do not be ashamed to do so. To reject Jesus Christ and His work on the cross is to reject God's perfect and only gift of
salvation and eternal life.

HERE'S YOUR CHANCE

Friend, here is your chance to get things right with God. The Bible says, If you confess with your mouth that Jesus Christ is Lord, and if you believe in your heart that God has raised Him from the dead, you shall be saved. For with the heart mankind believes unto righteousness, and with the mouth confession of salvation is made". Romans 10:9,10. So believe in your heart that these words from the Bible are true. Please consider what I am saying. I beg you with all my heart to place your faith in Christ right now. Tomorrow is promised to no one.

You see, I am not sharing this message to simply tell you an interesting story. Rather I want you to taste the goodness of God in my life, a man who was once a devil worshipper and a murderer, to show you that Jesus Christ is about forgiveness, hope and change.

I was involved in the occult and I got burned. I became a cruel killer and threw away my life as well as destroyed the lives of others. Now I have discovered that Christ is my answer and my hope. He broke the chains of mental confusion and depression that had me bound. Today I have placed my life in His hands. I only wish I knew Jesus before all these crimes happened - they would not have happened.
God bless you and thank you for reading this.

With Love in Christ,
David Berkowitz
March 1999

Dear Brother Mike,   March 21, 2002
     Thank you for the letter. I was both blessed and encouraged to hear from you, a fellow Christian, and how the Lord has called you to prison ministries, especially to the men and women who are on America's Death Rows. May the Lord continue to use you to touch many lives, and your labor of love for the Lord and His people is never in vain (1 Corinthians 15:58).
     I've never heard of Maranatha Baptist Bible College, but I'm glad they have a prison ministry. Please know that I am praying for you, too.
     I also want to order some videos for you, and I hope to do so (Lord willing) within the next several weeks. Maybe you will be able to use them in the facilities you go into, or at least show them at the Bible college to encourage the saints. For even many Christians need to be reminded that God truly longs to save even the worst of criminals, that NO person has ever done so much evil that they cannot be saved.
     My birthday is June 1, and I will be 49 years old. We have a vibrant church here and a chaplain who truly loves the Lord. The Lord has blessed us with an anointed choir. I help out where needed and the Lord has given me a ministry working with the "special needs" inmates.

These are the men who have various emotional or other coping problems. Many were homeless or addicted to drugs before they came to prison. Many spent years in and out of psychiatric and mental health facilities. I love working with these humble brothers.

I would really appreciate your prayers, brother Mike. For there is always a lot of spiritual warfare and many temptations I must face. We all have to face these things, of course. But the warfare has been very hard because, I was like the demon possessed man in Mark 5 and Luke 8, and my testimony is having an impact. So naturally I think the Devil has put me on his "Most Wanted" list.

Well let me get this into the mail. I've been hoping to answer your letter all this week, and now I have. I'm putting my website address at the bottom of this page. You can download the testimony or anything else anytime.

I also put my correct address at the top of the first page. God bless you, Mike.

    Yours in the Lord,
       David Berkowitz

P.S. Please pray for:
    Protection and safety
    That I will always be humble and thankful
    That the Lord will reach many more with my testimony
    My family to be saved
    For the President and the leadership of our nation
    For the gospel to spread in the prisons

http://wwww.inetworld.net/hutrcc/davidb.htm

Dear Brother Mike,   April 9, 2002

I have your letter of March 28th and it's great hearing from you. I'm so pleased to hear how the Lord has been prospering your life and ministry.

Yes, I've been a Christian since 1987 when the Lord called me out of darkness and brought me into his marvelous light. He definitely has not treated me as my sins deserve. Psalm 103:10 "He hath not dealt with us after our sins; nor rewarded us according to our iniquities."

Brother Mike, we have a good fellowship here with a Chaplain who is born again and a number of men who love the Lord. I have total gratitude in my heart for all our Lord Jesus Christ has done in my life and in the lives of my fellow prisoners.

Of course prison ministry is not easy. Much prayer is needed and much tactfulness. There are setbacks and disappointments, struggles and discouragement's…but there are also many wonderful victories. Prison ministry is a work of patience and a labor of love.

Thank you for sharing my testimony with a number of the staff as well as with your peers. I was thrilled to hear that someone is getting more tracts from Moments with the Book.

I will also include the website, and you can give it to anyone who would like to look up my testimony online or read any of my monthly journal, messages, about the Africa ministry, etc. I just want to encourage others that no one is beyond the reach of God's forgiveness. Also that, if He can use me, God can use anyone for His glory.

Yes, all of my family are unsaved. I pray dearly that they will one day (soon) embrace Jesus as their Messiah. Romans 10:1 "Brethren, my heart's desire and prayer to God for Israel is, that they might be saved." This is one of my favorite verses.

I have heard about Velma Barfield. I am not very familiar with her case. I do know, however, that she became a Christian while on Death Row and ministered to many people. She's home with Jesus now, and so is Karla Faye Tucker.

Mike, I know you have a full schedule. So I will end this letter. God bless you, and I hope you will have the videos within a couple more weeks. Use them for God's glory.
    Your friend in Christ,
    Bro. David

Luke 12:32 "Fear not, little flock; for it is your Father's good pleasure to give you the kingdom."

Dear Brother Mike,   April 25, 2002

I have your letter of April 15th which came in a large envelope along with several letters from some of your friends. Please thank the people who wrote. I was so encouraged by what they had to share and for their kindness. I only wish I could write back to them, but it is too much for me to handle.

Mike, I hope you received my letter which was dated April 9th. You see I sometimes have a problem with my mail. Letters that I would send out won't reach their destinations. Fortunately this doesn't happen all the time, but it happens often enough. And your letter of 4/15 did not mention getting my 4/9 letter. So the next time you write, please let me know if the letter was received or not. Thanks! This is a big help to me.

That was very encouraging about the Cook County Jail visit. The Lord is using you and the ministry team for His glory and to make an impact for the Lord. Your labor in Christ is never in vain in Him (1st Corinthians 15:58).

And what a great blessing to hear about your trip to Waupan. Thanks for passing out copies of the Son of Hope tract. This encouraged me.

Yes, I did hear about the book by L. Klausner. It came out a long time ago. I never met with or spoke to the author. This was back in a dark time. Praise the Lord, for the Bible says in John 8:36, "If the Son therefore shall make you free, ye shall be free indeed." What counts is being a "new creation" in Christ. 2nd Corinthians 5:17 "Therefore if any man be in Christ, he is a new creature: old things are passed away; behold, all things are become new."

To answer your question though, I don't think it would be possible for you to use anything out of the book, even what are alleged to be my old writings, because the book is under copyright. If it were up to me, you could use these things. I wouldn't mind at all. But there are those copyright laws, and I would assume that the publisher has to give a say so for you to use anything. Otherwise you could get into trouble without getting their permission. This is a big hassle, right?

Mike, you are more then welcome to use my letters as witnessing tools. Its all for God's glory. Feel free to pass the Son of Hope tracts around anywhere. You could leave a copy or two in a public library or in a Burger King.

And speaking of witnessing tools, I hope that by now you've received two different videos. <u>The Choice is Yours</u> should be coming up from Florida. <u>Forgiven for Life</u> should be arriving from Atlanta, Georgia.

Let me know what you think of them. Feel free to show them to anyone you want to. Use them for God's glory, and you never have to ask for my permission to use the tracts or videos. Everything belongs to the Lord as far as I'm concerned.

I'm praying for you, and don't forget to tell me if you got my 4/9 letter. Thanks!

>Your friend in Christ,
>Bro. David

> Psalm 100:5 "For the LORD is good; his mercy is everlasting; and his truth endureth to all generations."

Dear Brother Mike,   June 17, 2002

I hope this letter finds you doing well and enjoying your summer. I have your letter of April 30th. I was not able to answer it earlier. Bro, these past several months have not been easy for me. But the Lord is faithful and His grace has proven to be all sufficient all the time.

I have only continuous praise and gratitude in my heart for all that Jesus Christ has done for me, how He rescued me from the darkness and brought me into His marvelous light. I simply cannot comprehend God's love and why He would reach out to save such a wretch like I was. Nevertheless I am thankful that He did reach out to me, that Jesus washed away all my sins through His precious blood.

Mike, I am so very encouraged that you have been able to use the videos as well as give out the testimony. Thank you so much. For the Lord knows that if I could, I myself would be giving out the testimony and sharing my story of hope whenever I can. So feel free to pass out the tracts and do whatever the Lord puts in your heart.

That's great news about passing all the exams. The people who came to the Lord as a result of the prison and jail outreach, you will one day get to see them again in Heaven. God will reward you, even though I know we do not labor for rewards but simply because we love the Lord.

I can see you have such a heart for the Lord and for things like evangelism. This encourages me because I do not see such zeal in many Christians.

I am praying about your friendship with Joy. Yes, if you have to give her more space, do so. One of the things I am learning with all my years as a Christian is the value of patience. Patience is one of the fruits of the Spirit. God does bless and honor those who wait upon Him and wait for Him to put everything into place.

You asked what my favorite hymn is. I would have to say its Just as I Am.

My favorite book in the Bible? This is a tough one. I would have to say Esther or Ruth. These are my favorite stories and some of my favorite Bible characters in addition to Daniel, Jeremiah and John the Baptist.

Well let me get this in the mail. Don't forget to check out the website if you can for updates. Again, sorry for the delay.

        Your friend in Christ,
        Dave

Psalm 118:24 "This is the day which the LORD hath made; we will rejoice and be glad in it."

Dear Brother Mike,   July 6, 2002

I hope this letter finds you rejoicing in the Lord and trusting in Him for all things.

Today is the first cool day after what seemed to be several weeks of stifling heat and humidity. My cellblock was like an oven and sauna. I thank God for the lifting of the humidity and for the beautiful weather today.

I have your letter of June 24th. Thanks for the newsletter. I enjoyed the message from your Pastor on "What is a Fundamentalist?" I agree with him and, sadly, much of the "church" has indeed departed from the essential fundamentals of our faith.

And Mike, I was very surprised and blessed to find the testimony in the newsletter. Please thank Pastor Pallmann for allowing it to be printed. Chances are that many in the body of Christ are not even aware that I am a Christian today. There are many who simply never heard my testimony. Other, however, are very skeptical. But this is the way it goes. I always think of how Barnabus had to speak up for the apostle Paul and represent him before the other Christians in the early years of Paul's profession of faith in Jesus. Many were terrified of him and had a hard time believing that he was truly changed and transformed by the Lord. But we know the end of the story, and Paul truly was a "new creature" in Christ.

Brother Mike, I can see you have a big heart for sharing the gospel and evangelizing. This is encouraging to see a fellow Christian with such a heart. I say this because of the other infamous prisoners you're trying to reach out to.

I am sorry to hear about all the hassles you had with your clinical tests. I trust that by now everything's been resolved. I know, too, that the Lord will provide for you to get to Kenya, if it is His will. But it seems right now that He is using you, right where you are. I was happy to hear about all the people who are getting saved. Praise the Lord! His Word never returns to Him void.

I see that you deeply care about Joy. If she needs her space for now, then let her have it. I am sure you only tell her the right things from your heart. I am sure she appreciates your honesty.

And as for a visit, I would love to meet you one day. Let's trust in the Lord for the right timing. This August would not be the best, and there are reasons for my saying this. With the 25th anniversary coming up and the possibility of so much media stuff going on, I would rather hold off for a while until things quiet down. But of course my prayer is that the media as a whole will show little interest and I could get on with my life.

God bless you, brother Mike. I thank the Lord for your friendship. Keep the faith.

                Your brother in Christ,
                Bro. David

1st John 4:11 "Beloved, if God so loved us, we ought also to love one another."

Hi Brother Mike!   July 25, 2002

I pray that this letter finds you doing well and being encouraged by God's Word. Heaven and earth will pass away, but the Lord's Word shall endure forever. Jesus Christ the same yesterday, and to day, and forever.

Thanks for your letter of July 14th. I really do appreciate your Pastor going against the grain, so to speak, and printing my testimony in his church's Baptist Beacon. I hope the congregation accepted the testimony and that your Pastor was not unfairly criticized.

Today is a special blessing for me. In a little while, Lord willing, my testimony is going to be shared at the Gideons International Bible Convention in Louisville, Kentucky. This convention lasts several days. But on this day portions of one of my testimony videos is going to be shown to glorify the Lord.

It was a small Gideons KJV pocket New Testament that the Lord used to reach my hard heart. I thank God that, as I sit here in a prison cell, God is using my life for a good purpose to encourage members of the Gideons who are in attendance. They come from all countries. And to remind them that no one is beyond God's reach or the forgiveness that Jesus Christ offers. Hebrews 7:25 "Wherefore he is able also to save them to the uttermost that come unto God by him." This, by the way, is one of my favorite verses in the Bible as well as John 6:37 "All that the Father giveth me shall come to me; and him that cometh to me I will in no wise cast out." The Lord rejects no one unless they refuse His invitation for salvation.

Thanks, Mike, for telling me about some of the things you saw and heard about the parole hearing. I did not go to this hearing to seek parole, but only to apologize for the crimes I committed and for the lives I destroyed and the people I hurt. The parole commissioners took note of my remorse and sorrow. And I also got to share my faith in Christ and the positive things I've been doing with my life today-which really means what Christ is doing through my life. I told the parole board that I have much to be thankful for. But of course the media, for the most part, paid little attention to this.

Hey, I love your Ice Cream Truck job. I love ice cream. But your boss would never want a guy like me to work for him because I would eat up all the profits! Ha!

I'm glad things are going well for you. The Lord has been blessing your life and showing you favor.

I am also glad that you and Joy are getting along well. I know you're looking forward to seeing her again. Her missions trip to Poland must have been a blessing. It is a spiritually hungry land.

Well, maybe one day, if the Lord doesn't come in the months ahead, maybe during your winter break we could meet. But don't worry about it. God has a time for everything.

Oh, thanks for the tracts. They're very good. Keep the faith. My prayers are with you.

                Your brother in Christ,
                Bro. David

Delight thyself also in the Lord; and He shall give thee the desires of thine heart.
Psalm 37:4

Hi Mike!!!   September 9, 2002

It's great hearing from you, and by now you're settled back into MBBC.

That's great about your going to the Bill Rice Ranch. I have heard many good things about this place, and I am so glad to know that you want to get closer to the Lord. I have been going through the same situation. I am not satisfied at my own walk with the Lord. I just want more of Jesus, to know Him better and to truly love the Lord with all my heart, soul, mind and strength. I want to spend more time in His word.

Earlier today I was reading Psalm 42. The 1st verse says that "as the hart panteth after the water brooks, so panteth my soul after thee, O God." I want to be ready to meet Jesus. I want to please Him with my life.

Mike, thanks for telling me about the good and favorable comments concerning my testimony appearing in your church's newsletter. It was another blessing from the Lord! He has begun to use my testimony in even more ways.

Several weeks ago the 700 Club reaired the testimony I did with them back in 1997. Then on August 16th the Billy Graham radio program, "Decision Today", aired my testimony. How I thank the Lord. I feel so unworthy to even make mention of His name. then my friend Troy from Atlanta told me that the radio director told him that about one hundred people called in after the testimony was aired. I guess that at the end of the program they give out a toll free number for people to call in if they want to know more about Jesus and if they need prayer, etc. So I'm very blessed!

And I am also very blessed to have such a good friend and brother in Christ as you. I'm sorry to hear about the ice cream truck job. It brought me back to my childhood days when several different kinds of ice cream trucks would go up and down the streets in my old neighborhood in the Bronx. My favorite was a Bungalow Bar. I'm sure this was before your time. Then there was the Good Humor man, Mister Softee and Dairy Queen. Great times!

I will keep you and Joy in my prayers. Give your life to the Lord. He will work everything out. Be patient.

Mike, I also want to tell you that the website which has my testimony has changed. I will give you the new location at the bottom of the page.

I'm sure you're busy with your studies so I will end this letter now. Don't be in a hurry to write back. Focus on your school work. Bye for now.

    Your bro in Jesus,
        Bro. David

www.forgivenforlife.com

"And they were not able to resist the wisdom and the spirit by which he spake"
Acts 6:10

Hi Mike!,   October 1, 2002

    How's my brother in Christ doing today? It's Tuesday morning and I just dropped off the man I have to escort to his classroom. He is visually impaired and my job is to escort him through the hallways and throughout the prison. And of course I have many other tasks to do, too. It's the Lord who lives through us, bro. It is all by Jesus' strength and for His glory.

    I have your letter dated September 16th. You encourage me when I read how you're living for the Lord and how you long to serve Him. I am thrilled to see your emphasis on soulwinning. Many Christians have forgotten this calling and our Lord's Great Commission. We call Jesus Lord yet we do not do what He says. Surely there is something wrong with this picture! The church is to go out into all the world to bring the message of salvation. That you are faithful in doing this is an inspiration for me. Thank you, Mike.

    I'm glad to hear about your jail ministry. Thanks so much for handing out the Son of Hope tracts. You've become my feet and mouth, going where I cannot go and speaking what I cannot speak in person.

    I'm sorry that things did not work out with Joy. But you have your whole life ahead of you. The Lord will lead you to the right one. It does sound like this Josie girl is a nice person? You never know. Give things time.

    Your witnessing on State Street in Madison is great. Praise the Lord for that college freshman who came to the Lord. One plants the gospel seed, and another waters it with love and encouragement, and then God gives the increase (1st Corinthians 3:6).

I will pray for your dad for salvation and healing with the cancer. Did you really eat an ostrich egg? Where did you get that thing? Or are you kidding me?

God bless you, my friend and brother in the Lord. Keep the faith. And remember, patience is one of the fruits of the spirit.

Until next time...
    Your bro in the Lord,
        Bro. David

Dear Brother Mike,   November 1, 2002

I hope this letter finds you doing well and prospering in your studies and in your service to the Lord.

I have your letter dated October 15th. That's very encouraging about your work inside of the Cook County Jail. The Lord is using you, my brother.

I sure wish I could have gone with you. However I am grateful that you give out copies of my testimony when you have them available. Also, that you're handing out the tracts on State Street in Madison. And I pray that the two men you led to the Lord recently, M. Johnson and T. Reyes, will continue to grow in Christ and not turn back to sin.

You mentioned a book titled "Set Free" about Karla Faye Tucker. I never heard of this book and I have no idea where to get it. Maybe one day if it is the Lord's will I'll come across a copy of it.

Thankfully the sniper shootings have come to an end. I pray for the families who've lost a loved one and who are devastated. I likewise pray for the injured to recover as soon as possible.

As for your new friend Josie, trust in God. Things will work out. Wait on the Lord. It's fine to date. But simply make sure it is His will before you get into a serious and consuming relationship right now.

Mike, we'll see about a visit when the time comes. The Lord will make a way if it's His will. But let me know in advance as I have to work and need to make arrangements for another man to cover me on a certain day.

Well bro, God bless ya! Keep the faith. I am very tired now and need to take a break this weekend.

    Your brother in Christ,
        Bro. Dave

P.S. In case you want to get the Larry King transcript of my interview which aired on Oct. 26th, go here:
http://www.cnn.com/transcripts/0210/26/lklw.00.html
"Larry King Live Weekend."

A poem sent to David

A Tribute to God's Love
(The Son of Sam)

A disciple of the devil,
Was David Berkowitz.
To shed the blood of others
Was his passion and his wish.

Driven by a demon,
To murder still again,
A prisoner of the darkness,
Was the ruthless Son of Sam.

Satan was David's father,
The young man had no peace.
His mind had been tormented,
His soul had been deceived.

A vegetable rotting away,
Behind the prison walls.
Left to die in anguish,
Until the day that Jesus called.

David tried to take his life,
His pain became to great.
Another tried to slit his throat,
But God gave David grace.

Imagine here's a murderer,
Known as the Son of Sam,
This man thirsty of death and blood,
Is now God's little lamb.

David had a date with hell,
That he knew he deserved.
But a friend gave him a Bible,
And David read God's Word.

While reading in the Book of Psalms,
The Lord touched David's will.
Born again was David Berkowitz,
The Son of Sam was killed.

God took a convicted murderer,
And washed his sins away.
In heaven he's now innocent,
Of his violent yesterdays.

The blood that David shed,
Would haunt him day and night.
But the blood that Jesus shed for him,
Gave David back his life.

Praise You God Almighty,
Lord of Heaven and of Earth.
For setting guilty David free,
And giving him new birth.

Revenge it is craving,
That our sinful heart's demand.
But only God's forgiveness,
Makes a murderer His lamb.

Consecutive life sentences,
Behind the prison bars,
David now spends with a Friend,
Who has nail prints and scars.

God left His throne in Heaven,
And found David Berkowitz.
God wrapped His arms around him,
And David did not resist.

The demons stopped tormenting,
The moment David knew,
The King of Kings and Lord of Lords,
Would be his Savior too.

Condemned to die in prison,
For deeds done years before,
This saint of God named David,
Knows he'll walk through Heaven's doors.

Gary Lee Myers "The Poet of Truth"
7/14/99

Jeffrey Dahmer

Jeffrey's final statement to the court:

"Your Honor, it is over now. This has never been a case of trying to get free. I didn't ever want freedom. Frankly, I wanted death for myself. This was a case to tell the world that I did what I did, not for reasons of hate -- I hated no one. I knew I was sick or evil or both. Now I believe that I was sick. The doctors have told me about my sickness and now I have some peace. I know how much harm I have caused, and I tried to do the best that I could after the arrest to make amends, but no matter what I did, I could not undo the terrible harm I have caused. My attempt to identify the remains was the best that I could do and that was hardly anything. I feel so bad for what I did to those poor families, and I understand their rightful hate."

"I know I will be in prison for the rest of my life. I know that I will have to turn to God to help me get through each day. I should have stayed with God. I tried and failed and created a holocaust. Thank God that there will be no more harm that I can do. I believe that only the Lord Jesus Christ can save me from my sins."

"I have instructed Mr. Boyle to end this matter. I do not want to contest the civil case. I have told Mr. Boyle to finalize them if he can. If there is ever any money, I want it to go to the victim's families. I have talked to Mr. Boyle about other things that might help me ease my conscience in some way of coming up with ideas on how to make some amends with these families and I will work with him on that. I want to return to Ohio and quickly end that matter so I can put all this behind me and then come right back here and do my sentence."

"I decided to go through this trial for a number of reasons. One of the reasons was to let the world know that these were not hate crimes. I wanted the world of Milwaukee, who I deeply hurt, to know the truth of what I did. I didn't want unanswered questions. All of the questions have now been answered. I wanted to find out just what it was that caused me to be so bad and evil. But most of all, Mr. Boyle and I decided that maybe there was a way for us to tell the world that if there are people out there with these disorders maybe they can get some help before they end up being hurt or hurting someone. I think the trial did that."

"I take all the blame for what I did. I hurt many people. The judge in my earlier case tried to help me and I refused his help and he got hurt by what I did. I hurt those policemen in that Konerack matter and I shall forever regret causing them to lose their jobs. I hope and pray that they can get their jobs back because I know that they did their best and I just plain fooled them. For that I am so sorry. I know I hurt my probation officer who was really trying to help me. I am so sorry for that and for everyone else that I have hurt."

"I hurt my mother and father and stepmother. I love them all so very much. I hope they will find the same peace that I am looking for."

"Mr. Boyle's associates Wendy and Ellen have been wonderful to me, helping me through this worst of all times. I want to publicly thank Mr. Boyle. He didn't have to take this case, but when I asked him to help me find answers and to help others if I could, he stayed with me and went way overboard in trying to help me."

"Mr. Boyle and I agreed that it was never a matter of trying to get off, only a matter of which place I would be housed for the rest of my life. Not for my comfort, but for trying to study me in hopes of helping me in learning to help others who might have problems. I know I will be in prison. I pledge to talk to doctors who might be able to find some answers."

"In closing, I just want to say that I hope God has forgiven me. I know that society will never be able to forgive me. I know the families of the victims will never be able to forgive me for what I have done. I promise I will pray ever day to ask for their forgiveness when the hurt goes away, if ever. I have seen their tears and if I could give my life to bring their loved ones back I would do it. I am so very sorry."

"Your Honor, I know that you are about to sentence me. I ask for no consideration. I want you to know that I have been treated perfectly by the deputies who have been in your court and the deputies that work the jail. the deputies have treated me very professionally and I want everyone to know that. They have not given me special treatment."

"Here is a trust worthy saying that deserves full acceptance: Christ Jesus came into the world to save sinners, of whom I am the worst. But for that very reason, I was shown mercy so that in me, the worst of sinners, Christ Jesus might display his unlimited patience as an example for those who would believe in him and receive eternal life. Now to the King, Immortal, Invisible, the only God, be honor and glory forever and ever."

"I know my time in prison will be terrible, but I deserve whatever I get because of what I have done."

"Thank you, your Honor, and I am prepared for your sentence which I know will be the maximum. I ask for no consideration."

Could convicted mass murder Jeffrey Dahmer get to Heaven before you?

Jeffrey Dahmer will definitely go down in history as a very wicked man. Being a homosexual who abducted, raped, tortured, murdered and cannibalized his many victims, he is ranked among the worlds worst men in the minds of most. Now I want you imagine a difficult thing; that Dahmer went straight into the arms of Jesus the moment he died. "Impossible", you might snort with indignation! "Why this guy was a real sicko, an evil savage. The Devil incarnate! This boy will surely burn in hell for eternity!"

Well, I would like to tell you a true story about Dahmer which was reported in the "Christian Chronicle" and "The Daily Oklahoman" newspapers. A Christian lady named Mary Mott saw Dahmer on a TV show discussing his need for inner peace. Mott mailed a series of Bible lessons to Dahmer which he completed and mailed back to Mott. He thanked Mott and said he wanted to become a Christian. Through a series of events a Christian minister, Roy Ratcliff, went into the prison and studied the Bible with Dahmer. He was immersed in water for the remission of his sins on May 10, 1994. He continued to study the Bible every week in prison until the day of his murder, Nov 28, 1994. One TV report quoted Dahmer as saying that he was at peace with himself and God, just two weeks prior to his murder.

Now I am not playing down the horrendous sins that Dahmer committed. But the real question is; could Dahmer go to Heaven? Could God forgive him for what he did? I must admit that when I first heard this bizarre twist of events, that I had no problem believing God could forgive. My problem was believing that someone like Dahmer could truly repent of his sins.

The Jews on Pentecost asked Apostle Peter after he convicted them of murdering Jesus Christ, "What shall we do?" Peter replied to them, "Repent and be baptized in the name of Jesus for the remission of your sins" Acts 2:37-38. Which sin was worse? Dahmer's or the murder of the sinless Christ? God forgave 3000 souls of their sin of murdering Christ. "So then, those who had received Peter's word were baptized; and there were added that day about three thousand souls." Acts 2:41 The critical question is not whether God could forgive Dahmer, but whether Dahmer truly repented.

Apostle Paul was also guilty of murdering the innocent. He was primarily responsible for the stoning of Stephen in Acts 8. Later, after Paul was converted, he wrote of himself, "It is a trustworthy statement, deserving full acceptance, that Christ Jesus came into the world to save sinners, among whom I am foremost of all. And yet for this reason I found mercy, in order that in me as the foremost, Jesus Christ might demonstrate His perfect patience, as an example for those who would believe in Him for eternal life." 1 Tim 1:15-16 Paul was acutely aware that he had committed a terrible crime by murdering Stephen.

Will Dahmer go to Heaven? No one knows except God. It will be based upon the genuineness of Dahmer's repentance and conversion. But I would personally like to think he is. In fact I would like God to use Jeffery Dahmer as an example of His divine forgiveness. Perhaps God picks one notorious sinner who repented from each generation and holds him up and says, "If I can forgive Jeffery Dahmer, I can forgive anyone of any sin."

Imagine you have two men. One is a vile sinner, murderer and thief. The second was awarded the citizen of the year award and only has a little sin in his life. Which one is closer to God? Neither! They are both equally far away because it is the first sin that sends us to hell, not the number of sins or how bad the sins are we commit.

If Dahmer is saved, it only illustrates that God is not a respecter of persons, that God sees all sins as equal. Yet for many people they cannot even consider that Dahmer could be saved. That is because they mistakenly think that our salvation is based upon our good works rather than the unmerited favor of God. I call this misconception, "balance scale salvation". They think that as long as the good outweighs the bad that they will go to heaven. Well, not in God's eyes! For unless the citizen of the year truly repents of his one and only sin he ever committed and believes in Jesus as the eternal divine Savior, it is he who will go to hell and Jeffery Dahmer (with true repentance), will go to heaven!

Source: Steve Rudd, the author. The church was Church of Christ.
www.bible.ca

Charles Manson

"LOOK DOWN ON ME, YOU WILL SEE A FOOL. LOOK UP AT ME, YOU WILL SEE YOUR LORD. LOOK STRAIGHT AT ME, YOU WILL SEE YOURSELF."

Manson is one big enigma. He birthed a cult of drug-addicted people who killed. His birth certificate name is 'No Name Maddox'. He was the leader of the group labeled "The Family" back in the sixties. He spent most of his life in jail, prior to the murder spree. He used LSD. He masterminded the killing of actress, Sharon Tate and others. After each killing, his cult would write words using their victims' blood. Words such as: Pig, War, Death to Pig, Healter Skelter (Helter was misspelled), Rise. He is a racist. He carved a swastika into his forehead and so did some of his girl followers. He predicted that by the summer of 1969, blacks would go into white people's homes, take what they want, kill them and write things in blood. When blacks failed to live up to his own prophecy, he figured that they were too ignorant to do it so he had to show them (therefore the murders at the Tate home and the Labianca Home). He then felt that blacks would copy his crimes, and whites would mass together and fight them off. He planned for his cult to hide out in the California desert during the racial holocaust, and that Jesus Christ would come to Earth and make him and the Beatles angels. He often quoted from the Bible book of Revelations. He planned to skin Frank Sinatra alive while making him listen to his own music, then planned to sell his skin to make pouches out of. He plotted to castrate Richard Burton and to gouge out the eyes of Elizabeth Taylor. He wanted to send Susan Atkins (who physically committed the murders) to slit Tom Jones throat. It is hard to describe this man in my own words.

Below, are his own words from his last statement before the court at his 1970 trial.

THE TESTIMONY OF CHARLES MANSON
NOVEMBER 19, 1970

The Court: Do you have anything to say?
Manson: Yes, I do.

There has been a lot of charges and a lot of things said about me and brought against me and brought against the co-defendants in this case, of which a lot could be cleared up and clarified to where everyone could understand exactly what the family was supposed to have been, what the philosophies in regards to the families were, and whether or not there was any conspiracy to commit murder, to commit crimes, and to explain to you who think with your minds.

It is hard for you to conceive of a philosophy of someone that may not think.

I have spent my life in jail, and without parents.

I have looked up to the strongest father-figure, and I have always looked to the people in the free world as being the good people, and the people in the inside of the jail as being the bad people.

I never went to school, so I never growed up in the respect to learn to read and write so good, so I have stayed in jail and I have stayed stupid, I have stayed a child while I have watched your world grow up, and then I look at the things that you do and I don't understand.

But maybe the girls and women in your world outside ... Being by yourself for such a long time when you do get out you appreciate things that people don't even see, you walk over them every day.

Like in jail you have a whole new attitude or a whole different way of thinking.

I don't think like you people. You people put importance on your lives.

Well, my life has never been important to anyone, not even in the understanding of the way you fear the things that you fear, and the things you do.

I know that the only person I can judge is me.

I judge what I have done and I judge what I do and I look and live with myself every day.

I am content with myself.

If you put me in the penitentiary, that means nothing because you kicked me out of the last one. I didn't ask to get released. I liked it in there because I like myself.

I like being with myself.

But in your world it's hard because your understanding and your values are different.

These children that come at you with knives, they are your children. You taught them. I didn't teach them. I just tried to help them stand up.

Most of the people at the ranch that you call The Family were just people that you did not want, people that were alongside the road, that their parents had kicked them out or they did not want to go to Juvenile Hall, so I did the best I could and I took them up on my garbage dump and I told them this that in love there is no wrong.

You make your children what they are. I am just a reflection of every one of you.

I sit and I watch you from nowhere, and I have nothing in my mind, no malice against you and no ribbons for you.

But you stand and you play the game of money. As long as you can sell a newspaper, some sensationalism, and you can laugh at someone and joke at someone and look down at someone, you know.

I can't dislike you, but I will say this to you. You haven't got long before you are all going to kill yourselves because you are all crazy.

And you can project it back at me, and you can say that it's me that cannot communicate, and you can say that it's me that don't have any understanding, and you can

say that when I am dead your world will be better, and you can lock me up in your penitentiary and you can forget about me.

But I'm only what lives inside of you, each and every one of you. These children, they take a lot of narcotics because you tell them not to. Any child you put in a room and you tell them, "Don't go through that door," he never thought of going through that door until you told him to go through the door. You go to the high schools and you show them pills and you show them what not to take, how else would they know what it was unless you tell them?

And then you tell them what you don't want them to do in the hopes they will go out and do it and then you can play your game with them and then you can give attention to them because you don't give them any of your love.

You only give them your frustration; you only give them your anger; you only give them the bad part of you rather than give them the good part of you.

But it's okay, it's all okay. It doesn't really make any difference because we are all going to the same place anyway. It's all perfect. There is a God. He sits right over here beside me. That is your God. This is your God.

But let me tell you something; there is another Father and he has much more might than you imagine.

If I could get angry at you I would try to kill every one of you. If that's guilt, I accept it.

I have killed no one and I have ordered no one to be killed.

I may have implied on several occasions to several different people that I may have been Jesus Christ, but I haven't decided yet what I are or who I am.

I was given a name and a number and I was put in a cell, and I have lived in a cell with a name and a number.

I don't know who I am.

I am whoever you make me, but what you want is a fiend; you want a sadistic fiend because that is what you are.

You are not you, you are just reflections, you are reflections of everything that you think that you know, everything that you have been taught.

I have ate out of your garbage cans to stay out of jail.

I have wore your second-hand clothes.

I have accepted things and given them away the next second.

I have done my best to get along in your world and now you want to kill me, and I look at you and I look how incompetent you all are, and then I say to myself, "You want to kill me, ha, I'm already dead, have been all my life!"

I've lived in your tomb that you built.

I did seven years for a thirty-seven dollar check. I did twelve years because I didn't have any parents.

I say, "If there was ever a devil on the face of this earth I am him."

And he's got my head anytime he wants it, as all of you do too, anytime you want it.

Sometimes I think about giving it to you. Sometimes I'm thinking about just jumping on you and let you shoot me. Sometimes I think it would be easier than sitting here.

If I could I would jerk this microphone out and beat your brains out with it because that is what you deserve, that is what you deserve.

I live in my world, and I am my own king in my world, whether it be a garbage dump or if it be in the desert or wherever it be. I am my own human being. You may restrain my body and you may tear my guts out, do anything you wish, but I am still me and you can't take that.

You can kill the ego, you can kill the pride, you can kill the want, the desire of a human being.

You can lock him in a cell and you can knock his teeth out and smash his brain, but you cannot kill the soul.

You never could kill the soul. It's always there, the beginning and the end. you cannot stop it, it's bigger than me. I'm just looking into it and it frightens me sometimes.

My reality is my reality, and I stand within myself on my reality.

I was working on cleaning up my house, something Nixon should have been doing. He should have been on the side of the road picking up his children. But he wasn't. He was in the White House sending them off to war.

"You live for each others' opinion and you have pain on your face and you are not sure what you like, and you wonder if you look okay."

And I look at you and I say, "Well, you look alright to me," you know, and you look at me and you say, "Well, you don't look alright to me,"

When you were out riding your bicycles I was sitting in your cell looking out the window and looking at pictures in magazines and wishing I could go to high school and go to the proms, wishing I could go to the things you could do, but oh so glad, oh so glad, brothers and sisters, that I am what I am.

In my mind I live forever, and in my mind I have always lived forever.

I am only what you made me. I am only a reflection of you.

I have done everything I have always been told. I have mopped the floor when I was supposed to mop the floor. And I have swept when I was supposed to sweep.

I was smart enough to stay out of jail and too dumb to learn anything. I was too little to get a job there, and too big do to something over here.

I have just been sitting in jail thinking nothing. Nothing to think about.

Everybody used to come in and tell me about their past and their lives and what they did. But I could never tell anybody about my past or what my life was or what I did because I have always been sitting in that room with a bed, a locker, and a table. So, then it moves on to awareness: how many cracks can you count in the wall? It moves to where the mice live and what the mice are thinking, and see how clever mice are.

In the penitentiary you live with it, with constant fear of death, because it is a violent world in there, and you have to be on your toes constantly.

So, it is not without violence that I live. It is not without pain that I live.

The words go in circles.

You can say everything is the same, but it is always different. It is the same, but it is always different. You can "but" it to death. You can say, "You are right, but, but, but."

Where I am from, if you snitch, you leave yourself open to be killed.

I could never snitch because I wouldn't want someone to kill me.

But I know this: that in your own hearts and your own souls, you are as much responsible for the Vietnam War as I am for killing these people.

I knew a guy that used to work in the stockyards and he used to kill cows all day long with a big sledgehammer, and then go home at night and eat dinner with his children and eat the meat that he slaughtered. Then he would go to church and read the bible, and he would say, "That is not killing." And I look at him and I say, "That doesn't make any sense, what you are talking about?"

Then I look at the beast, and I say, "Who is the beast?"

I am the beast.

I am the beast.

I am the biggest beast walking the face of the earth. I kill everything that moves. As a man, as a human, I take responsibility for that. As a human, it won't be long, and God will ask you to take responsibility for it. It is your creation. You live in your creation. I never created your world, you created it.

You create it when you pay taxes, you create it when you go to work, then you create it when you foster a thing like this trial.

Only for vicarious thrills do you sell a newspaper and do you kowtow to public opinion. Just to sell your newspapers. You don't care about the truth. You take another Alka-Seltzer and another aspirin and hope that you don't have to think of the truth and you hope that you don't have to look at yourself with a hangover as you go to a Helter Skelter party and make fun of something that you don't understand.

(The Judge asks Manson to stick to the point.)

When no one wanted to go out in front and fight, I would go out and fight. When no one else wanted to clean the toilets, I would go and clean them.

People would see me and they would see what I do and see the example that I set. They see, when I am cleaning out a cesspool, that I am happy and smiling and making

a game of it. Like I was on a chain gang somewhere once upon a time and they come and pass the water. I make a game out of it, or I make a pleasure out of a job. We turn it into a magical mystery tour.

We speed down the highway in a 1958 automobile that won't go but fifty, and an XKE Jaguar goes by, and I state to Clem, "Catch him Clem, and we'll rob him or steal all of his money," you know. And he says, "What shall we do?" I say, "Hit him on the head with a hammer." We magical mystery tour it.

Then Linda Kasabian gets on the stand and says: "They were going to kill a man, they were going to kill a man in an automobile."

To you, it seems serious. But like Larry Kramer and I would get on a horse and we would ride over to Wichita, Kansas, and act like cowboys. We make it a game on the ranch.

Like, Helter Skelter is a nightclub. Helter Skelter means confusion. Literally. It doesn't mean any war with anyone. It doesn't mean that those people are going to kill other people. It only means what it means. Helter Skelter is confusion.

Confusion is coming down fast. If you don't see the confusion coming down fast around you, you can call it what you wish.

It is not my conspiracy. It is not my music. I hear what it relates. It says, "Rise!" It says, "Kill!" Why blame it on me? I didn't write the music.

I am not the person who projected it into your social consciousness, that sanity that you projected into your social consciousness, today.

Because there is nothing here to worry about, nothing here to think about, nothing here to be confused over. My house is not divided. My house is one with me, myself.

It is a pretty hideous thing to look at seven bodies, one hundred and two stab wounds.

The prosecutor, or the doctor, gets up and he shows how all the different stab wounds are one way, and then how all the different stab wounds are another way; but they are the same stab wounds in another direction.

I know what I know and nothing and no one can take that from me.

You can jump up and scream, "Guilty!" and you can say what a no good guy I am, and what a devil, fiend, eeky-sneaky slimy devil I am. It is your reflection and you're right, because that is what I am. I am whatever you make me.

Murder? Murder is another question. It is a move. It is a motion. You take another's life. Boom! and they're gone. You say, "Where did they go?" They are dead. You say, "Well, that person could have made the motion." He could have taken my life just as well as I took his.

If a soldier goes off to the battlefield, he goes off with his life in front. He is giving his life. Does that not give him permission to take one? No. Because then we bring our soldiers back and try them in court for doing the same thing we sent them to do. We train them to kill, and they go over and kill, and we prosecute them and put them in jail because they kill. If you can understand it, then I bow to your understanding. But in my understanding I wouldn't get involved with it.

My peace is in the desert or in the jail cell, and had I not seen the sunshine in the desert I would be satisfied with the jail cell much more over your society, much more
over your reality, and much more over your confusion, and much more over your world, and your word games that you play.

I have been in a cell with a guy eighty years old and I listened to everything he said. "What did you do then?" And he explains to me his whole life and I sat there and listened, and I experienced vicariously his whole being, his whole life, and I look at him and he is one of my fathers. But he is also another one of your society's rejects.

Where does the garbage go, as we have tin cans and garbage alongside the road, and oil slicks in your water, so you have people, and I am one of your garbage people. I am one of your motorcycle people. I am one of what you want to call hippies. I never thought about being a hippie. I don't know what a hippie is.

A hippie is generally a guy that's pretty nice. He will give you a shirt and a flower, and he will give you a smile, and he walks down the road. But don't try to tell him nothing. He ain't listening to nobody. He got his own thoughts. You try to tell him something, and he will say, "Well, if that's your bag."

I don't care what you believe. I know what I am. You care what I think of you? Do you care what I think of you? Do you care what my opinion is? No, I hardly think so. I don't think that any of you care about anything other than yourselves because when you find yourself, you find that everyone is out for themselves anyway.

The only thing you can prove is what you can prove to yourselves, and you can sit here and build a lot in that jury's mind, and they are still going to interject their personalities on you. They are going to interject their inadequate feelings; they are going to interject what they think. I look at the jury and they won't look at me. So I wonder why they won't look at me. They are afraid of me. And do you know why they are afraid of me? Because of the newspapers.

You projected fear. You projected fear. You made me a monster and I have to live with that the rest of my life because I cannot fight this case. If I could fight this case and I could present this case, I would take that monster back and I would take that fear back. Then you could find something else to put your fear on, because it's all your fear.

You look for something to project it on and you pick a little old scroungy nobody who eats out of a garbage can, that nobody wants, that was kicked out of the penitentiary, that has been dragged through every hellhole you can think of, and you drag him up and put him into a courtroom.

You expect to break me? Impossible! You broke me years ago. You killed me years ago. I sat in a cell and the guy opened the door and he said, "You want out?"

I was released from the penitentiary and I learned one lesson in the penitentiary, you don't tell nobody nothing. You listen. When you are little you keep your mouth shut, and when someone says, "Sit down," you sit down unless you know you can whip him, and if you know you can whip you stand up and whip and you tell him to sit down.

Well, I pretty much sat down. I have learned to sit down because I have been whipped plenty of times for not sitting down and I have learned not to tell people something they don't agree with. If a guy comes up to me and he says, "The Yankees are the best ball team," I am not going to argue with that man. If he wants the Yankees to be the best ball team, it's okay with me, so I look at him and I say, "Yeah, the Yankees are a good ball club." And somebody else says, "The Dodgers are good." I will agree with that; I will agree with anything they tell me. That is all I have done since I have been out of the penitentiary. I agreed with every one of you. I did the best I could to get along with you, and I have not directed one of you to do anything other than what you wanted to do.

Now in death you might find peace, and soon I may start looking in death to find my peace.

There's been a lot of tank about a bottomless pit. I found a hole in the desert that goes down to a river that runs North underground, and I call it a bottomless pit, because where could a river be going North underground? You could even put a boat on it. So I covered it up and I hid it and I called it "The Devil's Hole" and we all laugh and we joke about it. You could call it a Family joke about the bottomless pit. How many people could you hide down in this hole?

Or would it be a conspiracy for your wife to mention to you twenty times a day, "You know, you're going blind, George, you know how your eyes are, you're just going blind; we pray to God and you're going blind, and you're going blind." And she keeps telling the old man he's going blind until he goes blind.

Is that a conspiracy?

Is it a conspiracy that the music is telling youth to rise against the establishment because the establishment is rapidly destroying things? Is that a conspiracy? Where does conspiracy come in? Does it come in that?

I have showed people how I think by what I do. It is not as much what I say as what I do that counts, and they look at what I do and they try to do it also, and sometimes they are made weak by their parents and cannot stand up. But is that my fault? Is it my fault that your children do what they do?

Hippie cult leader; actually, hippie cult leader, that is your words. I am a dumb country boy who never grew up. I went to jail when I was eight years old and I got out when I was thirty-two. I have never adjusted to your free world. I am still that stupid, corn-picking country boy that I always have been.

The Court: Have you completed your statement, Mr. Manson?

Manson: You see, you can send me to the penitentiary, it's not a big thing. I've been there all my life anyway. What about your children? These are just a few, there is many, many more coming right at you.

The Court: Anything further?

Manson: No.

We're all our own prisons, we are each all our own wardens and we do our own time. I can't judge anyone else. What other people do is not really my affair unless they approach me with it.

Prison's in your mind ... Can't you see I'm free?

Manson is now in his sixties and receives more mail than any other prison inmate in the United States. He is also very hard to reach. I have attempted to contact him but it was to no avail.

God is in the business of changing lives around. Perhaps one day Manson will accept Jesus Christ as his Lord and Savior and we will get to see this man changed. It's amazing to know that God loves Charles Manson as much as he loves you and I. Manson has a soul and it will spend eternity somewhere. The question is where.

Charlie Manson B-33920, 4A 4R-23
P. O. Box 3476
Corcoran, CA 93212

Timothy McVeigh

A Copy of Timothy McVeigh's last statement:

Final Written Statement of Timothy McVeigh

Out of the night that covers me,
   Black as the Pit from pole to pole,
I thank whatever gods may be
   For my unconquerable soul.

In the fell clutch of circumstance
   I have not winced nor cried aloud.
Under the bludgeonings of chance
   My head is bloody, but unbowed.

Beyond this place of wrath and tears
   Looms but the Horror of the shade,
And yet the menace of the years
   Finds, and shall find, me unafraid.

It matters not how strait the gate,
   How charged with punishments the scroll,
I am the master of my fate;
   I am the captain of my soul.

June 11, 2001

Biblical Old Testament Death Penalty Sins

There are forty-two death-penalty sins in the Old Testament:
-Murder - Gen. 9:6; Ex. 21:12-14,20,23; Lev. 24:17,21; Num. 35:16-34; Deut. 19.
-Failing to circumcise - Gen. 17:14; Ex. 4:24,25.
-Eating leavened bread during feast of unleavened bread - Ex. 12:15,19.
-Smiting Parents - Ex. 21:15.
-Kidnapping - Ex. 21:16; Deut. 24:7.
-Cursing Parents - Ex. 21:17; Lev. 20:9.
-Negligence with animals that kill - Ex. 21:28-32.
-Witchcraft - Ex. 22:18.
-Bestiality - Ex. 22:19; Lev. 18:23-29; 20:15,16.
-Idolatry - Ex. 22:20.
-Making holy anointing oil - Ex. 30:33.
-Putting holy anointing oil on strangers - Ex. 30:33.-
-Making the holy perfume - Ex. 30:38.
-Defiling the Sabbath - Ex. 31:14.
-Working on the Sabbath - Ex. 35:2.
-Eating the flesh of the peace offerings in uncleanness - Lev. 7:20,21.
-Eating the fat of sacrifices - Lev. 7:25.
-Killing sacrifices other than at the door of the tabernacle - Lev. 17:1-9.
-Eating blood - Lev. 17:10-14.
-Incest - Lev. 18:6-29; 20:11-22.
-Eating sacrifices at the wrong time - Lev. 19:5-8.
-Consecration of children to idols - Lev. 20:1-5.
-Spiritualism - Lev. 20:6,27.
-Adultery - Lev. 20:10; Deut. 22:22-30.
-Sodomy/Homosexuality - Lev. 20:13.
-Relationship with a menstruous woman - Lev. 20:18.
-Whoredom - Lev. 21:9; Deut. 22:21,22.
-Sacrilege - Lev. 22:3.
-Refusing to fast on day of atonement - Lev. 23:29.
-Working on atonement - Lev. 23:30.
-Blasphemy - Lev. 24:11-16.
-Failure to keep the Passover - Num. 9:13.
-Presumptuous - Num. 15:30,31.

-<u>Gathering firewood on the Sabbath</u> - Num. 15:32,36.
-<u>Failure to purify self before worship</u> - Num. 19:13,20.
-<u>False prophecy</u> - Deut. 13:1-18; 18:20.
-<u>Leading men away from God</u> - Deut. 13:6-18.
-<u>Stubbornness and rebelliousness</u> - Deut. 21:18-23.
-<u>Gluttony</u> - Deut. 21:20-23.
-<u>Drunkenness</u> - Deut. 21:20-23.
-<u>Backbiting</u> - Deut. 17:2-7.
-<u>False dreams and visions</u> - Deut. 13:1-18.

"What States Kill You & What States Don't"

There are currently 38 states with the death penalty: Alabama, Florida, Louisiana, New Hampshire, Oregon, Virginia, Arizona, Georgia, Maryland, New Jersey, Pennsylvania, Washington, Arkansas, Idaho, Mississippi, New Mexico, South Carolina, Wyoming, California, Illinois, Missouri, New York, South Dakota, Colorado, Indiana, Montana, North Carolina, Tennessee, Connecticut, Kansas, Nebraska, Ohio, Texas, Delaware, Kentucky, Nevada, Oklahoma and Utah.

Twelve Jurisdictions are without death penalty statutes: Alaska, Hawaii, Iowa, Maine, Massachusetts, Michigan, Minnesota, North Dakota, Rhode Island, Vermont, West Virginia and Wisconsin.

"Texas Leads the Way (facts & figures)"

Texas Death Row Facts:

Cost per Day per Offender in Texas: $53.15 (based on FY2000) Texas leads the nation in the number of executions since the death penalty was reinstated in 1976. Texas, California and Florida have the largest Death Row populations.

Additional Execution Information: Death Row was located in the East Building of the Huntsville Unit from 1928 to 1952. From 1952 until 1965, the electric chair was located in a building by the East Wall of the Huntsville Unit. The men on Death Row were moved from the Huntsville Unit to the Ellis Unit in 1965. Death Row remained at the Ellis Unit until 1999. In 1999, the TDCJ began moved Death Row to the Terrell Unit. Death Row offenders are housed separately in single-person cells measuring 60 square feet, with each cell having a window. Death Row offenders are also recreated individually. Offenders on Death Row receive a regular diet, have access to reading, writing, and legal materials. Depending upon their custody level, some Death Row offenders are allowed to have a radio. Offenders on Death Row do not have regular TDCJ-ID numbers, but have special Death Row numbers.

Hanging was means of execution between 1819 and 1923. The State of Texas authorized the use of the electric chair in 1923, and ordered all executions to be carried out by the State in Huntsville. Prior to 1923, Texas counties were responsible for their own executions.

The State of Texas executed the first offender by electrocution on 2/8/1924. Charles Reynolds from Red River County was executed. On that same date, four additional offenders, Ewell Morris, George Washington, Mack Matthews, and Melvin Johnson were executed.

The state of Texas executed brothers on six occasions:
-Frank & Lorenzo Noel electrocuted 7/3/1925.
-S.A. & Forest Robins electrocuted 4/6/1926.
-Oscar & Mack Brown electrocuted 7/1/1936.
-Roscoe & Henderson Brown electrocuted 5/6/1938.
-Curtis 7/1/1993 & Danny 7/30/1993 Harris (both by lethal injection).
-Jessie 9/16/1994 & Jose 11/18/1999 Gutierrez (both by lethal injection).

One of the most notorious offenders to be executed was Raymond Hamilton, member of the "Bonnie and Clyde" gang. He was sentenced from Walker County and executed on May 10, 1935, for murder. Hamilton and another man had escaped from Death Row, only to be captured and return to Death Row. The State of Texas executed the last offender by electrocution on 7/30/1964. Joseph Johnson from Harris County was executed. A total of 361 inmates were electrocuted in the State of Texas.

When the U.S. Supreme Court declared capital punishment "cruel and unusual punishment" on June 29, 1972, there were 45 men on Death Row in Texas and 7 in county jails with a death sentence. The Governor of Texas commuted all of the sentences to life sentences, and Death Row was clear by March 1973.

In 1973, revision to the Texas Penal Code once again allowed assessment of the death penalty and allowed for executions to resume effective 1/1/1974. Under the new statute, the first man (John Devries) was placed on Death Row on 2/15/1974. Devries committed suicide 7/1/1974 by hanging himself with bed sheets. The State of Texas adopted lethal injection as means of execution in 1977. The State of Texas executed the first offender by lethal injection on 12/7/1982. Charlie Brooks of Tarrant County was executed for the kidnap/murder of a Fort Worth auto mechanic.

Effective January 12, 1996, close relatives and friends of the deceased victim were allowed to witness executions.

Shortest Time on Death Row

1-Joe Gonzales #999177 was on Death Row 252 days and executed on 9/18/96.
2-Steven Renfro #999229 was on Death Row 263 days and executed on 2/9/98.

Longest Time on Death Row

1-Excell White #511 was on Death Row for 8982 days (24 years) and was executed on 3/30/99.
2-Sammie Felder, Jr. #550 was on Death Row for 8569 days (23 years) and was executed on 12/15/99.

The average age of executed offenders is 39 years old.

Youngest at Time of Execution
1-Jay Pinkerton #686 was only 24 when he was executed on 5/15/1986.
2-Jesse De La Rosa #713 was only 24 when he was executed on 5/15/1985.

Oldest at Time of Execution
1-Clydell Coleman #968 was executed at the age of 62 on 5/5/1999.
2-Betty Beets #810 was executed at the age of 62 on 2/24/2000.
Source: www.tdcj.state.tx.us/index.htm 9/5/01

Texas Capital Offenses:
    The following crimes are Capital Murder in Texas: murder of a public safety officer or firefighter. Murder during the commission of kidnapping, burglary, robbery, aggravated sexual assault, arson, or obstruction or retaliation. Murder for remuneration. Murder during prison escape. Murder of a correctional employee. Murder by a state prison inmate who is serving a life sentence of any of five offenses (murder, capital murder, aggravated kidnapping, aggravated sexual assault, or aggravated robbery). Multiple murders. Murder of an individual
under six years of age.
Source: www.tdcj.state.tx.us/index.htm 9/5/01

Executions of females since 1976:
    <u>Seven female offenders executed since 1976</u>
-Velma Barfield in North Carolina on November 2, 1984
-Judy Buenoano in Florida on March 30, 1998
-Karla Faye Tucker in Texas on February 3, 1998
-Betty Lou Beets in Texas on February 24, 2000
-Christina Riggs in Arkansas on May 2, 2000
-Wanda Jean Allen in Oklahoma on January 11, 2001
-Marilyn Plantz in Oklahoma on May 1, 2001

The financial cost:
    The price paid, on average, for each one of the capital punishment cases from beginning to the execution, is around $500,000 to $4 million. The taxpayers of Suffolk County and Long Island New York State paid

$2.5 million for the capital murder trial of Robert Shulman, who was sentenced to death on May 6, 1999. Because prosecutors sought the death penalty, the trial was 3.5 times more expensive than if the death penalty had not been sought. The cost was more than double what it would have cost to keep Shulman, 45, in prison for 40 years. The public cost of Shulman's sentence will continue to climb throughout his incarceration. (Newsday, 7/12/99)

"100% True Inmate Stories"

I Die At Midnight

"And there were also two other, malefactors, led with him to be put to death. And when they were come to the place, which is called Calvary, there they crucified him, and the malefactors, one on the right hand, and the other on the left. And one of the malefactors which were hanged railed on him, saying, If thou be Christ, save thyself and us. But the other answering rebuked him, saying, Dost not thou fear God, seeing thou art in the same condemnation? And we indeed justly; for we receive the due reward of our deeds: but this man hath done nothing amiss. And he said unto Jesus, Lord, remember me when thou comest into thy kingdom. And Jesus said unto him, Verily I say unto thee, To day shalt thou be with me in paradise."
Luke 23:32-33, 39-43

When you read this, I'll be dead. But don't be alarmed at hearing from a dead man. For now, as I begin this story, I'm very much alive. It's Tuesday September 9, 1947. Midnight Thursday I am scheduled to die for murder. Sitting here in my cell in Cook County Jail, I've been doing a lot of thinking. Some of my thoughts-a warning to criminals-were published in "a note to tough guys" in today's Chicago Tribune.

This afternoon I read the note for a radio broadcast. But that was really just part of my story.

The real story, I feel, lies in the fact that I don't mind talking about dying. I'm a Negro, just 23 years of age, but I'm ready to go you see. Why, I am ready to meet God. I'm really happy. Just this week I had a dream that I will carry with me to the chair. I was on my way to Heaven. Jesus was with me. But I was taking four steps to His two. He asked me why I was going so fast. I told Him I was eager to get there. Then I was there, surrounded by numerous angels.

Some folks might think that's strange talk from a man who came to jail an atheist. But that's just the way that I feel. You'll under stand better when I tell you how I met God early one morning.

But first, take a glance at my past. Seven years ago I was a stickup man, head of my own gang of tough guys. There were eight of us. One was Earle Parks, dubbed Smiley, because he would kill you with a smile on his face. Another was Charles Jones known as Pretty Boy because he was a nice looking guy. The others: Herbert Liggins, known as Hop-a-long because he had a bad leg. William Lee was called "Wild Bill" and Charles Hill was known as the Colorado Kid. Clyde Bradford was so dark that we called him Blue. The Wheeler was Percy Bellmar. We nicknamed him that because he was a good driver, my number one wheeler. All are in prison, except for Parks, and he died for murder.

They called me "Little Gaither the Money Waster and Woman Chaser." I tried to act the "Big Shot," always flashing a big roll-sometimes two or three grand.

I started all this when I was just a kid. My folks tried to get me to go to Sunday School and church. More than once they gave me a quarter to go with my younger sisters. But I never went. Instead I'd make them promise not to tell, and then I'd go to a movie. I'd stay in the show most of the day and tell my folks that I'd gone to church. They didn't know the difference.

Crime was in me and movies I saw helped give me ideas. I got some good tips on "how to do it." I remember when I saw the movie, "I Stole a Million," I sat there wishing I'd been the guy who got the million.

I decided on a boxing career because I thought I was a tough and could care for myself. It would beat working, I figured. I was one of the best fighters in my class for a while. I turned pro in 1938 and fought a middleweight, and ended up in the light-heavy division. Jimmy Bevins was the only man ever to knock me out.

At 18 I was in the Illinois State Training School for Boys, for armed robbery. In October 1941 eight of us made a break but the following month I found myself resentenced to Joliet penitentiary. I had life for a Chicago park murder, but got out on parole in 1946. It looks as if that would have been a lesson to me, but it wasn't.

Within six months, after I was out, I was leading another gang. That lasted until February 9. That night three of us held up Max Baren, 49, in his liquor store on Chicago's West Side. Baren reached for a gun. I yelled at him to put the gun down, but he meant business. I knew it was us or him. So I shot Baren and killed him. We ran out with the money, only $300 which I later gave to the other guys. I went to New York, then to Atlanta, where police nabbed me.

Then weeks later I stood in a Chicago court. "...sentences you to die..." the judge said sternly.

And thus I went to Death Row.

Not long after I was placed behind the bars last March 23, a woman of my own race-Mrs. Flora Jones of Olivet Baptist Church-invited me to attend a prisoners' gospel service. I was playing cards with some other fellows at the time, and laughed at her. "Why, I don't even believe there's a God." I boasted, and went on playing cards, the woman still pleading with me. Actually I felt so sinful, that I dint want to know about God even if He existed. So I ignored her.

Suddenly something she was saying caught my attention. "If you don't believe in God," she called from outside the bars, "just try this little experiment. Before you go to sleep tonight ask Him to awaken you at any time; then ask Him to forgive you of your sin." She had real faith. It got a hold of me.

I didn't go to the service, but I decided I would try the experiment that night.

"God," I mumbled as I lay on my cot, "Wake me up at 2:45, if you're real."

Outside it was wintery. Windows on the inside were frosted. For the first few hours I slept soundly, then my sleep became restless. Finally I was wide awake. I was warm and sweating, although the cell was cool. All was quiet except for the heavy breathing of several prisoners and the snoring of a man near by. Then I heard footsteps outside my cell. It was a guard, making his regular check. As he was passing, I stopped him. "What time is it?" I asked.

He looked at his pocket watch. "Fifteen to three."

"That's the same as 2:45, ain't it?" I asked, my heart taking a sudden leap.

The guard grunted and passed on. He didn't see me climb from my cot and sink to my knees. I don't remember just what I told God, but I asked him to be merciful tome, an evil murderer and sinner. He saved me that night, I know. I've believed on His Son Jesus ever since.

I'd promised a whipping to another prisoner the next day. That morningi went to him. He backed off. "I don't want to fight you; you used to be a boxer," he said.

"I don't want to fight," I said. "I just came to see you." Several prisoners had gathered for a fight and were disappointed.

But God had saved me from my sins: why should I want to fight? Later it was whispered around that I was putting on an act, trying to get out of going to the chair.

My case did later come up before the Illinois Supreme Court, but they upheld the death sentence. Sure, that jolted me some, but I haven't lost faith in God. I know He will go with me. So, you see, I'm really not afraid.

Before I die I want to leave one last message for the young people. Start serving the Lord while you're young. Grow up this way and it'll keep you straight. Once crime gets a hold of you, it's hard to stop. Just like the habits of smoking and drinking: if they once get a hold of you, you can't quit.

Yes, I'll be dead when you read this, but please take my advice: "the wages of sin is death; but the gift of God is eternal life through Jesus Christ our Lord." Romans 6:23. I found out it's true.

Pete Tanis, a prison gate missionary from Pacific Garden Mission accompanied Ernest Gaither to the electric chair. His description of the prisoner's last hours follows.

I was admitted to Ernest's cell about an hour before midnight. The atmosphere seemed charged, and the guards who stood about his cell kept talking to keep his mind off the midnight journey. But things they said were strained and meaningless, like the things you say when you don't know what to say.

As I entered, Ernest smiled and greeted me. A chaplain was reading to him from the Bible. He gave me the book and asked me to read. I selected the first chapter of Philippians. Ernest leaned forward intently as I read: "For to me to live is Christ, and to die is gain. For I am in a strait betwixt two, having a desire to depart, and to be with Christ; which is far better." (Phil. 1:21,23).

This seemed to be a favorite to him, along with the twenty-third Psalm. He got a lot of comfort from Psalm 23:4. "Yea, though I walk through the valley of the shadow of death, I will fear no evil: for thou art with me; thy rod and thy staff they comfort me." He quoted this from memory, as the clock ticked away the last hour of his life. Outside, the guards listened quietly, some wet eyed.

About 11:30 we had a song service. Ernest said he'd like to sing "When the Roll is Called Up Yonder" and soon the corridors rang with music as a Negro's high tenor voice rang out above the off-key voices of the guards.

As the last strains of another song: "Just A Little Talk With Jesus" were dying away, guards came with clippers to give a hair cut to the man with the tenor voice.

Just before midnight Ernest prayed, "God," he began softly, "when I first came here, I hated these guards. But now, God, I love 'em-O God, I love everybody." Then he prayed for people he made suffer: for his mother, that the Lord would bless her. "And Lord," he continued, "I'm not going to die of electrocution-I'm just going to sit in a chair and go to sleep."

A moment later a black hood was placed on his head and he began the last mile. At each side were guards, both noticeably nervous. Ernest sensed it.

Now 75 witnesses looked on as unsteady hands strapped the hooded figure into the big black chair, accentuated against a stainless steel floor. Then for two minutes-hours, it seemed-an attendant worked feverishly on a defective electrode.

Finally, at 12:03 a.m., the first of the three electrical shocks flashed through his body.

By 12:15 five doctors had paraded up, and one by one they confirmed his death.

But I knew that the real Ernest Gaither still lived-only his body was dead. As I left the jail, I thought of the verse he liked so well: "For to me to live is Christ, and to die is gain."

Christ died for our sins according to the scriptures; And that he was buried, and that he rose again the third day according to the scriptures." First Corinthians 15:3,4.

Jerry McAuley
The History of a River Thief

I do not attempt this record of my life from any feeling of vainglory, or any craving for notoriety. Neither is it because I have had a remarkable history. I have been a great sinner, and have found Jesus a great Savior; and this is why I would tell my story, that others may be led to adore and seek the blessed Friend who saved, and has thus far kept me by his grace.

I was born in Ireland. Our family was broken up by sin, for my father was a counterfeiter, and left home to escape the law, before I knew him. I was placed at a very early age in the family of my grandmother, who was a devout Catholic.

I was never taught or sent to school, but left to have my own way; to roam about in idleness, doing mischief continually, and suffering from the cruel and harsh treatment of those who had care of me.

At the age of thirteen I was sent to this country, to the care of a married sister in New York City. Here I ran errands for the family, and assisted my brother-in-law in his business, and soon, by the practice of little tricks, became well used to dishonesty, and was a great rogue as one of my years could be. After a while I felt I could live by my own wits, and left my sister's home to take care of myself. I took board in a family in Water Street, where were two young men with whom I associated myself in business. I earned what I could, and stole the rest, to supply my daily wants.

We had a boat, by means of which we boarded vessels in the night, stealing whatever we could lay our hands on. Here I began my career as a river thief. In the daytime we went up into the city and sold our ill-gotten goods, and with the proceeds dressed up, and then spent our time, as long as our money lasted, in the vile dens of Water Street, practicing all sorts of wickedness. Here I learned to be a prize fighter, and by degrees, rapid degrees, rose through all the grades of vice and crime, till I became a terror and a nuisance in the Fourth Ward.

I was only nineteen years of age when I was arrested for highway robbery-a child in years but a man of sin. I knew nothing of the criminal act which was charged to my account; but the rum sellers and inhabitants of the Fourth Ward hated me for all of my evil ways and were glad to get rid of me. So they swore the robbery on me, and I couldn't help myself. I had no friends, no advocate at court, and without any just cause I was sentenced to fifteen years in State Prison. I burned with vengeance; but what could I do! I was handcuffed and sent in the cars to Sing-Sing.

That ride was the saddest hour of my life. I looked back on my whole past course, on all my hardships, my misery and sins, and gladly would I have thrown myself out before the advancing train, and ended my life. It was not sorrow for sin that possessed me, but a heavy weight seemed to press me down when I thought of the punishment. I had got to suffer for my wrong-doings, and an indignant, revengeful feeling for the injustice of my sentence. Fifteen years of hard labor in a prison to look forward to, and all for a crime I was innocent of. I knew I had done enough to condemn me, if it were known; but others, as bad as I, were at liberty, and I was suffering the penalty for one who was at that hour roaming at will, glorying in his lucky escape from punishment, and caring nothing for the unhappy dog who was bearing it in his stead. How my heart swelled with rage, and then sank like lead, as I thought of my helplessness in the hands of the law, without a friend in the world.

I concluded, however, before I reached the end of that short journey, that my best way was to be obedient to prison rules, do the best I could under the circumstances, and trust that somebody would be raised up to help me.

When I arrived at the prison-I shall never forget it-the first thing that attracted my attention was the sentence over the door: "The way of transgressors is hard."

Though I could not read very well, I managed to spell that out. It was a familiar sentence, which I had heard many times. All thieves too, that it is out of the Bible. It is a well-worn proverb in all the haunts of vice, and one confirmed by daily experience. And how strange it is that, knowing so well that the way is hard, the transgressors will still go in it.

But God was more merciful to me than man. His pure eyes had seen all my sin, and yet he pitied and loved me, and stretched out his hand to save me. And his wonderful way of doing it was to shut me up in a cell with those heavy stone walls. There's many a one beside me who will have cause to thank God forever that he was shut up in a prison.

I was put to the carpet weaving business, and for two years not a word could be said against me. All the keepers and guards spoke well of me. I minded my work, and was quiet and orderly. I used to say my prayer-The Lord's prayer-every day, from a feeling that it was right to say it, and that in some way or other it would do me good. I tried to learn to read and write, and improved very much, especially in reading. Then I got cheap novels and read, to pass away the time. I read many of them. It was all the recreation I had, and diverted my mind from my dreary surroundings. I was supplied with them constantly, and, in consequence, my head was filled with low and wicked thoughts. I took a fancy, from some of the remarkable stories I read, that I might by some good fortune by and by effect my escape from prison, and then my heart would fill up with murderous intentions toward the man that put me in.

After this I was sick, and suffered a good deal for two or three years, and became at times uneasy and intractable. Then I had to suffer severe punishment; but punishment never did me a particle of good, it only made me harder and harder.

I had been in prison four or five years, one Sunday morning, I went with the rest to service in chapel. I was moody and miserable. As I took my seat, I raised my eyes carelessly to the platform, and who should I see there beside the chaplain but a man Orville Gardner, who had been for years a confederate in sin. "Awful Gardner" was the name by which I had always known him. Since my imprisonment he had been converted, and was filled with desire to come to the prison, that he might tell the glad story to the prisoners. I had not heard he was coming, and could not have been more surprised if an angel had come down from Heaven. I knew him at the first glance, although he was so greatly changed from his old rough dress and appearance. After the first look I began to question in my mind if it was he after all, and thought I must be mistaken; but the moment he spoke I was sure, and my attention was held fast.

He said that he did not feel that he belonged on the platform, where the ministers of God and good men stood to preach the gospel to the prisoners; he was not worthy of such a place. So he came down and stood on the floor in front of the desk, that he might be among the men. He told them it was only a little while since he had taken off the stripes which they were then wearing; and while he was talking his tears fairly rained down out of his eyes. Then he knelt down and prayed, and sobbed and cried, till I do not believe there was a dry eye in the whole crowd. Tears filled my eyes, and I raised my hand slowly to wipe them off, for I was ashamed to have my companions or the guards see me weep; but how I wished I was alone, or that it was dark, that I might give way to my feelings unobserved. I knew this man was no hypocrite. We had been associated in many a dark deed and sinful pleasure. I had heard oaths and curses, vile and angry words from his mouth, and I knew he could not talk as he did then unless some great, wonderful change had come to him. I devoured every word that fell from his lips, though I could not understand half I heard. One sentence, however, impressed me deeply, which he said was a verse from the Bible. The Bible! I knew there was such a book, that people pretended it was a message from God; but I had never cared for it, or read one word in it. But now God's time had come, and he was going to show me the treasures that were hid in that precious book.

I went back to my cell. How dreary is Sunday in prison! After the morning service in the chapel, the prisoners are marched back to their cells, taking their plate of dinner with them as they pass the dining hall, and the rest of the day is spent in solitude. Oh, those long dismal hours! I had generally tried to have a novel on hand, but that day I had none. What

I had heard was ringing in my ears, and the thought possessed me to find the verse which had so struck me. Every prison cell is supplied with a Bible; but alas! Few of them are used. Mine I had never touched since the day I entered my narrow apartment, and laid it away on the ventilator. I took it down, beat the dust from it, and opened it. But where to turn to find the words I wanted I knew not. There was nothing to do but to begin at the beginning, and read it until I came to them. On and on I read. How interested I grew! It seemed better than any novel I had ever read, and I could scarcely leave it to go to sleep. I became so fascinated, that from that day on it was my greatest delight. I was glad when I was released from work, that I might get hold of my Bible; and night after night, when daylight was gone, I stood up by my grated door to read by the dim light which came from the corridor. I had supposed it to be dry, dead thing-a book only fit for priests and saints, but now, whenever I could get a chance to communicate with my mates in the workshop, I told them that it was a "splendid thing, that Bible."

I never found that verse. I had forgotten it in my new interest in the book. But I found a good many verses that made me stop and think. Then I read the whole book through again, and I liked it better the second time than I did the first. The book of Revelation particularly astonished me. I tried to believe, but I could not understand it.

I was resting one night from reading, walking up and down thinking what a change religion had made in Gardner, when I began to have a burning desire to have the same. I could not get rid of it; but what could I do? Something within me said, "Pray." I couldn't frame a prayer. he voice said, " Don't you remember the prayer of the publican, 'God be merciful to me a sinner'!" "But that will not save me as Gardner's does him," I thought; "It does not keep me from my sins." There was a struggle in my mind. "If I send for the priest," I said to myself, "he will tell me I must do a penance, say so many prayers, and do something for mortification, and such as that. If I ask the chaplain, he will tell me to be sorry for my sins, and cry to God for forgiveness. Both can't be right." The voice within said, "Go to God He will tell you what is right."

What a struggle I went through! I knew I ought to pray; but if there had been ten thousand people there I couldn't have been more ashamed to do it than I was there all alone. I felt myself blushing. Every sin stared me in the face. I recollected the "Whosoever" in the Bible. "That means you," I urged; "everything but a murderer, and that many a time in my will." The struggle did not seem all my own; it was as if God was fighting the devil for me. To every thought that came up there came a verse of scripture. I fell on my knees; and was so ashamed I jumped up again. I fell on my knees again, and cried out for help, and then, as ashamed as before, I rose again. I put it off for that time and went to bed.

This conflict went on for three or four weeks. It was fearful. I wonder now at the long-suffering mercy of my God. I wonder that the Holy Spirit was not grieved to depart from me forever. But at last the Lord sent a softness and a tenderness into my soul, and I shed many tears. Then I cried unto the Lord, and began to read the Bible on knees.

The Sunday services seemed to do me no good. They were dry and dead to me. Once in a while a man full of the Holy Ghost preached for us, and at such times I got little help. About that date Miss D. began to visit the prison, and I was sent for one day to meet her in the library. This young lady had learned that I was seeking the Savior, and had asked to see me. She talked with me, and then knelt down to pray. I felt ashamed, but I knelt beside her. I looked through my fingers and watched her. I saw her tears fall. An awe I cannot describe fell on me. It seemed dreadful to me, the prayer of that holy woman. It made my sins rise up till they looked to me as if they rose clean up to the throne of God, and it appeared to me as if they troubled God, they rose up so high. What should I do? Oh, what can a poor sinner do when there is nothing between him and God but a life of dark, terrible sin?

That night I fell on my knees on the hard stone floor in my cell, resolved to stay there, whatever might happen, till I found forgiveness. I was desperate. I felt just like the words of the hymn,

"Perhaps he will admit my plea,
Perhaps will hear my prayer,
But if I perish I will pray,
And perish only there."

I prayed, and then I stopped; I prayed again, and stopped; but still I continued kneeling. My knees were rooted to those cold stones. My eyes were closed, and my hands tightly clasped, and I was determined I would stay so till morning, till I was called to my work; "and then," said I to myself, "if I get no relief, I will never, never pray again." I felt that I might die, but I didn't care for that.

All at once it seemed as if something supernatural was in my room. I was afraid to open my eyes. I was in agony, and the sweat rolled off my face in great drops. Oh, how I longed for God's mercy! Just then, in the very height of my distress, it seemed as if a hand was laid upon my head, and these words came to me: "My son, thy sins, which are many, are forgiven." I do not know if I heard a voice, yet the words were distinctly spoken to my soul. Oh, the precious Christ! How plainly I saw him, lifted on the cross for my sins! What a thrill went through me. I jumped from my knees; I paced up and down my cells. A heavenly light seemed to fill it; a softness and a perfume like the fragrance of sweetest flowers. I did not know if I was living or not. I clapped my hands and shouted, "Praise God! Praise God!"

One of the guards was passing along the corridor, and called out, "What's the matter!" "I've found Christ," I answered; "My sins are all forgiven. Glory to God!" He took out a paper from his pocket and wrote the number of my cell, and threatened to report me in the morning. But I didn't care for that. My soul was all taken up with my great joy. But the next morning nothing happened to me, and I think the Lord made him forget it. What a night that was! I shall surely never forget the time when the Lord appeared as my gracious Deliverer from sin.

Jerry McAuley won many of his fellow inmates to Christ. His life was so transformed that the governor gave him a pardon. Upon release he fell back into sin. In 1872 McAuley opened the Helping Hand Mission for Men (later called the Water Street Mission). Multitudes were soundly converted. Many became pastors, preachers, missionaries and rescue mission workers. He is credited with directly or indirectly influencing the start of 1,000 rescue missions around the world. When he died at the age of 45 he was one of the most influential Christian men in New York. Thousands mourned his passing.

43 Years Of Loneliness

Cranston, R.I., February 2nd. Biennin Crovagreer, 75, who served 43 years as a convicted murderer without a single visitor or a letter from the outside world, died yesterday at the state infirmary, where he was transferred in 1941 under conditional pardon.

He spent 26 years in a bed, hopelessly paralyzed.

Crovagreer, a Polish immigrant, was sentenced to life imprisonment in 1912 for the shooting to death of Joseph Brigham at West Kingston, R.I., after a violent argument. He had neither relatives nor friends. Death was his only visitor.

My, what a tragedy! Here was a young man, only 32 years old, who spent the majority of his life in prison because of a wrathful moment.

There was a quarrel, violent blows and curses flew-then whipped out a pistol-a shot, and lifelong tragedy.

43 long years behind bars. 43 long years of hard beds and prison fare. 43 long years of companionship with murderers, thieves, perverts and human derelicts. Never a day or night of peace. Never an hour of human love. Not even a moment of those long years without the guilt-ridden conscience condemning him for taking the life of a fellow man.

In all those 43 years not one friend visited him. Not one of his former acquaintances ever wrote him a letter. Forsaken and forgotten he lived the lonely existence of the doomed.

Jail is no joke! Many young people today have the attitude that they can play with the law and steal, rape, or even murder, and get away with it. But you can't. Sooner or later the heavy hand of the law falls upon you and then it is too late. Then, you must pay the penalty. Crime never pays.

At 75 years of age Biennin Crovagreer had his first visitor. Death visited hi; and his soul went out into eternity. We don't know if he was a saved man or not, but if he was not, his soul is today with the rest of the Christ rejecting sinners, in Hell.

Hell is God's penitentiary for sinners. Those who break God's laws and live and die in sin go there after death. There, their soul is to spend eternity separated from God. Then, their soul will long for God's forgiving righteousness but they shall not find him. There will be multitudes in Hell, but every one of them will be lonely; separated from God, being punished from sin. Every unforgiven sin must be punished.

"For we know him that hath said, Vengeance belongeth unto me, I will recompense, saith the Lord. And again, The Lord shall judge his people. It is a fearful thing to fall into the hands of the living God." Hebrews 10:30-31

This was written to you. Unless you have your soul cleansed from the stain and guilt of sin before you die, your soul will go to Hell awaiting the judgment of God. Do you want this? Certainly, no more than you would want to exchange places with Biennin Crovagreer and spend even 43 years in prison.

Well, there is good news for you. There is a way to escape Hell. God has provided a way for you if you take it.

The Man Who Refused The Pardon

"Seek ye the LORD while he may be found, call ye upon him while he is near: Let the wicked forsake his way, and the unrighteous man his thoughts: and let him return unto the LORD, and he will have mercy upon him; and to our God, for he will abundantly pardon." Isaiah 55:6-7

On December 6, 1829 two men, George Wilson and James Porter, robbed a United States mail carrier in Pennsylvania. Both men were subsequently captured and tried. On May 1, 1830 both men were found guilty of six indictments which included robbery of the mail "and putting the life of the driver in jeopardy." On May 27th both George Wilson and James Porter received their sentences: execution and hanging. The sentences were to be carried out on July 2nd, 1830.

By today's standards, this sentences seems very harsh. Remember, no one was killed in their crimes. In the earlier days of American history the justice system more closely followed Biblical principles.

The system was both swift: "Because sentence against an evil work is not executed speedily, therefore the heart of the sons of men is fully set in them to do evil." Ecclesiastes 8:11. And harsh: "Whoso sheddeth man's blood, by man shall his blood be shed: for in the image of God made he man." Genesis 9:6.

James Porter was executed on schedule. George Wilson was not. Shortly before the set date a number of influential friends pleaded for mercy to the president of the United States, Andrew Jackson, on behalf of their friend.

President Jackson issued a formal pardon. The charges resulting in the death sentence were completely dropped. Wilson would only have to serve a prison term of twenty years for his other crimes.

Incredibly George Wilson refused the pardon!

According to the official report, The United States Versus George Wilson (Peters 7 Report Sections 150-163) Wilson was returned to court as they attempted to "force" the pardon on him. It is recorded that George Wilson chose to: "…Waive and decline any advantage or protection which might be supposed to arise from the pardon referred to…" Wilson also stated that he "…had nothing to say, and that he did not wish in any manner to avail himself in order to avoid sentence…"

The case reached the Supreme Court. The Attorney-General made the following comments: "The court cannot give the prisoner the benefit of the pardon, unless he claims the benefit of it...It is a grant to him: it is his property; and he may accept it or not as he pleases."

Chief Justice John Marshall wrote the following decision: "A pardon is an act of grace, proceeding from the power entrusted with the execution of the laws, which exempts the individual, on whom it is bestowed, from the punishment the law inflicts for a crime he has committed...

A pardon is a deed, to the validity of which delivery is essential; and delivery is not completed without acceptance. It may then be rejected by the person to whom it is tendered; and if it be rejected, we have discovered no power in a court to force it on him.

It may be supposed that no being condemned to death would reject a pardon, but the rule must be the same in capital cases and in misdemeanors."

In other words, George Wilson committed a crime. He was tried and found guilty. He was sentenced to be executed. A presidential decree granted him a full pardon. But George Wilson chose rather to refuse that pardon. The courts concluded that the pardon could not be forced upon him.

George Wilson chose to Die!

Now that you have read George Wilson's amazing story, you are probably saying: "How could anyone refuse a pardon for the death sentence? The man was a fool!"

What would you say if someone told you that you too were refusing a pardon? A pardon that would result in you spending eternity in the presence of God rather than eternal separation from God in Hell.

The Bible plainly teaches that all of us are sinners. "But we are all as an unclean thing, and all our righteousnesses are as filthy rags; and we all do fade as a leaf; and our iniquities, like the wind, have taken us away." Isaiah 64:4

"The heart is deceitful above all things, and desperately wicked: who can know it?" Jeremiah 17:9

"As it is written, There is none righteous, no, not one." Romans 3:10

"Now we know that what things soever the law saith, it saith to them who are under the law: that every mouth may be stopped, and all the world may become guilty before God. Therefore by the deeds of the law there shall no flesh be justified in his sight: for by the law is the knowledge of sin." Romans 3:19-20

"For all have sinned, and come short of the glory of God" Romans 3:23

"If we say that we have no sin, we deceive ourselves, and the truth is not in us." 1st John 1:8

"Who can say, I have made my heart clean, I am pure from my sin?" Proverbs 20:9

God must punish sinners. "...the soul that sinneth, it shall die." Ezekiel 18:4

"Wherefore, as by one man sin entered into the world, and death by sin; and so death passed upon all men, for that all have sinned." Romans 5:12

"For the wages of sin is death..." Romans 6:23

The death spoken of here is the second death. "And death and hell were cast into the lake of fire. This is the second death. And whosoever was not found written in the book of life was cast into the lake of fire." Revelation 20:14-15

"But the fearful, and unbelieving, and the abominable, and murderers, and whoremongers, and sorcerers, and idolaters, and all liars, shall have their part in the lake which burneth with fire and brimstone: which is the second death." Revelation 21:8

But God has provided a pardon. "Cast away from you all your transgressions, whereby ye have transgressed; and make you a new heart and a new spirit: for why will ye die, O house of Israel? For I have no pleasure in the death of him that dieth, saith the Lord GOD: wherefore turn yourselves, and live ye." Ezekiel 18:31-32

"The Lord is not slack concerning his promise, as some men count slackness; but is longsuffering to us-ward, not willing that any should perish, but that all should come to repentance." 2nd Peter 3:9

"If we confess our sins, he is faithful and just to forgive us our sins, and to cleanse us from all unrighteousness." 1st John 1:9

Will you receive or reject the pardon? "He that believeth on him is not condemned: but he that believeth not is condemned already, because he hath not believed in the name of the only begotten Son of God." John 3:18

"He that believeth on the Son hath everlasting life: and he that believeth not the Son shall not see life; but the wrath of God abideth on him." John 3:36

Look closely at these last two verses.

1-"He that Believeth" is not only "not condemned" but "hath everlasting life."

2-"He that believeth not" is "condemned already" and "shall not see life."

3-Why is he (any person) "condemned already" and has " the wrath of God" abiding on him? Simply because "he hath not believed in the name of the only begotten Son of God."

To "believe" means to depend upon or rely on much like a drowning person must believe (depend upon) a lifeguard to save his life.

When we believe on the name of Jesus Christ we are depending upon the authority of God the Son to do what He has promised in His Word, the Bible.

"But as many as received him, to them gave he power to become the sons of God, even to them that believe on his name" John 1:12

"…All that the Father giveth me shall come to me; and him that cometh to me I will in no wise cast out." John 6:37

"And you hath he quickened, who were dead in trespasses and sins." Ephesians 2:1

Will you receive the pardon?

1-Do you believe you are a guilty sinner? (Romans 3:10, 19-20, 23)

2-Do you believe God punishes sinners? (Ezekiel 18:4; Revelation 21:8)

3-Do you believe Jesus Christ died to save you? "But God commendeth his love toward us, in that, while we were yet sinners, Christ died for us. Much more then, being now justified by his blood, we shall be saved from wrath through him." Romans 5:8-9

"Forasmuch as ye know that ye were not redeemed with corruptible things, as silver and gold, from your vain conversation received by tradition from your fathers; But with the precious blood of Christ, as of a lamb without blemish and without spot." 1st Peter 1:18-19

4-Will you ask the Lord Jesus to save you? "For whosoever shall call upon the name of the Lord shall be saved." Romans 10:13

George Wilson rejected the president's pardon and lost his human life. Will you reject God's pardon as provided by Jesus Christ and loose your eternal life?

"There is therefore now no condemnation to them which are in Christ Jesus, who walk not after the flesh, but after the Spirit." Romans 8:1

Salvation

In this day it's not often that someone offers an absolutely free gift. Yet here is the most wonderful and precious free gift you can ever get. Someone else has already paid it for.

The gift is ETERNAL LIFE in a GLORIOUS HEAVEN. It is difficult for men to accept the thought of this being a free gift. Man wants to earn everlasting life.

The Holy Bible says in Ephesians 2:8-9 "For by grace are ye saved through faith; and that not of yourselves: it is the gift of God: Not of works, lest any man should boast." The Bible also says in Romans 6:23 "For the wages of sin is death; but the gift of God is eternal life through Jesus Christ our Lord."

A gift is not something we earn or work for. We receive gifts out of love. In fact, "Grace" means: unmerited or unearned favor." If we work for something it is not a gift, but a wage. There is only one spiritual wage a person can obtain…

The only wages we receive from God is Hell. The wages of sin is death. The book of James 1:15 says "Then when lust hath conceived, it bringeth forth sin: and sin, when it is finished, bringeth forth death." 2nd Thessalonians 1:8 "In flaming fire taking vengeance on them that know not God, and that obey not the gospel of our Lord Jesus Christ."

Receiving wages should be an idea we replace with receiving the gift. "For the wages of sin is death; but the gift of God is eternal life through Jesus Christ our Lord." We earn death in Hell, but God gives us Heaven through Jesus Christ.

The Lord Jesus Christ paid for this gift with His own dear shed blood on the cross. Hebrews 9:22 "without shedding of blood is no remission." 1st John 1:7 "the blood of Jesus Christ his Son cleanseth us from all sin." Romans 5:8 "But God commendeth his love toward us, in that, while we were yet sinners, Christ died for us."

Receive this absolutely free gift today! Come to God in humble prayer. Admit your guilt as a sinner before a Holy God; turn to God from your sin by faith (repent). Ask God to save you through the Lord Jesus Christ. John 1:12 "But as many as received him, to them gave he power to become the sons of God, even to them that believe on his name." Romans 10:13 "For whosoever shall call upon the name of the Lord shall be saved." 2nd Corinthians 6:2 "behold, now is the accepted time; behold, now is the day of salvation."

From Timothy McVeigh to famous movie stars, warehouse workers to musicians. The gift of salvation is for everyone, including you!

God is on Death Row. He is in each jail cell with each condemned prisoner. It's their choice if they choose to acknowledge His presence or not.

Any questions regarding Heaven or Hell or any questions regarding salvation, Jesus Christ, the Bible or becoming a born-again Christian may be sent directly to the current president of the Maranatha Baptist Bible College Jail/Prison Society:

Prison Society President
Maranatha Baptist Bible College
745 West Main Street
Watertown, WI 53094

Reaching Out

As of October 1st in 2004 there was 3,471 death row inmates. The actual numbers will be higher due to some inmates being sentenced to death in more then one state.

These inmates are the same as us. They have the same rage we do and the same love. They are us but on a different route in life. No two people on this earth are the exact same inside and out. These people just made mistakes and some are even innocent. Let the one who has no sin cast the first stone. What if you are placed in a situation like this one day? Could you handle it alone?

To request the name and address of someone on Death Row, write to:

Death Row Outreach
745 West Main Street
Watertown, WI 53094

I don't know how to say it, but somehow it seems to me;
That maybe we are stationed where God wants us to be.
That the little place I am filling is the reason for my birth,
And just to do the work I do, He sent me down to earth.
If God had wanted otherwise I reckon He's have made
Me just a little different, of a worse or better grade.
And since God knows and understands all things on land and sea;
I fancy that he placed me here just where he wanted me.
Sometimes I get to thinking as my labors I review;
That I should like a higher place, with greater things to do.
But I come to the conclusion when my envying is stilled;
That the post to which God sent me is the post he wanted filled.
So I plod along and struggle in the hope, when day is through;
That I'm really necessary, to the things God wants to do.
And there isn't any service I can give which I should scorn;
For it may be just the reason, God allowed that I be born!
Author Unknown

2nd Corinthians 1:9-10
"<u>But we had the sentence of death in ourselves,</u> *that we should not trust in ourselves, but in God which raiseth the dead: Who delivered us from so great a death, and doth deliver: in whom we trust that he will yet deliver us.*"

Printed in the United States
35179LVS00005B/1-24